T0402687

PRAISE FOR
DRESSED, STYLED, AND DOWN THE AISLE

"Julie was inarguably the first person to realize that a wedding-wardrobe stylist was as important as a red-carpet stylist. Her services, including day-of-wedding troubleshooting, have proven to be invaluable for so many of my clients, and I'm so glad she wrote this book."

—MARCY BLUM, renowned wedding and event planner

"The original bridal stylist, Julie has tips, tricks, and unparalleled insights that have helped thousands of brides find their dream dress, and I am thrilled she is now sharing her wisdom with the world."

—PRESTON BAILEY, globally celebrated event designer and author of *Preston Bailey: Designing with Flowers*

"*Dressed, Styled and Down the Aisle* gives brides access to the tips, wisdom, and insights of the original bridal stylist. It is packed full of insider information and is a must-have resource for brides. Knowledge is confidence. Get ready to look and *feel* beautiful."

—REEM ACRA, renowned fashion designer

"In *Dressed, Styled, and Down the Aisle*, Julie compassionately walks brides through the often overwhelming world of wedding fashion, drawing on personal experiences to offer invaluable insights. With a commitment to inclusivity and self-love, this book is not just a guide to finding the perfect dress but also a heartfelt companion, empowering brides everywhere to embrace their unique style and confidently navigate the entire wedding wardrobe journey."

—LYNN EASTON, founder and creative director, Easton Events

"I can confidently say that, as my co-conspirator of style since 2012, Julie is the go-to authority on bridal fashion. *Dressed, Styled, and Down the Aisle* is a bridal masterpiece for a stylish and stress-free journey down the aisle! It is filled with insider tips, expert guidance, and a dash of humor—a must-have for every stylish bride on her journey to the altar!"

—BRYAN RAFANELLI, chief creative officer, Rafanelli Events

"As a photographer, I know the dress selection can be one of the most important decisions for the big day. Julie Sabatino has created a "how-to" guide on calming the storm that is wedding dress shopping. Through her amazing expertise, inclusivity for all brides, and clear and precise guidance, Julie helps simplify the entire process. Not only will this book make finding a dress easier, it will also help the bride find a dress that has the elements they have dreamed of, along with the style that suits their body shape and personal style."

—JOSE VILLA, fine art wedding photographer

"I have known Julie and her team for many years and have watched her style brides of all shapes and sizes and with varying needs—and I can confidently say that the service she provides is invaluable. Her wonderful mix of compassion, insight, patience, and humor quickly puts brides at ease, and her extensive industry knowledge helps them to quiet the noise and find their dream dress in record time. It's such a gift that she's chosen to write this book. With her tips and tricks, everyone can become a Stylish Bride."

—MINDY WEISS, Founder of Mindy Weiss Party Consultants

DRESSED, STYLED, *and* DOWN *the* AISLE

Becoming a Stylish Bride

Julie Sabatino

Founder of The Stylish Bride®

This publication is designed to provide accurate and authoritative information in regard to the subject matter covered. It is sold with the understanding that the publisher and author are not engaged in rendering legal, accounting, or other professional services. Nothing herein shall create an attorney-client relationship, and nothing herein shall constitute legal advice or a solicitation to offer legal advice. If legal advice or other expert assistance is required, the services of a competent professional should be sought.

Published by Greenleaf Book Group Press
Austin, Texas
www.gbgpress.com

Distributed by Greenleaf Book Group

For ordering information or special discounts for bulk purchases, please contact Greenleaf Book Group at PO Box 91869, Austin, TX 78709, 512.891.6100.

Design and composition by Greenleaf Book Group and Sheila Parr
Cover design by Greenleaf Book Group and Sheila Parr
Cover photo by Christian Oth Studio
Illustrations by Hwi Illust
Photo credits appear on page 243, which serves as an
extension of the copyright page.

Publisher's Cataloging-in-Publication data is available.

Print ISBN: 979-8-88645-137-5

eBook ISBN: 979-8-88645-138-2

To offset the number of trees consumed in the printing of our books, Greenleaf donates a portion of the proceeds from each printing to the Arbor Day Foundation. Greenleaf Book Group has replaced over 50,000 trees since 2007.

Printed in China on acid-free paper

24 25 26 27 28 29 30 31 10 9 8 7 6 5 4 3 2 1

First Edition

To Annmarie and Teddy

Always stay true to yourself and celebrate what makes you shine. I love you.

To Mike

None of this would have been possible without your never-ending encouragement and our long walks in the woods. Thank you for always believing in me. I love you.

CONTENTS

CHURCH OF
ST. VINCENT
Sunday
Saturday Vigil
Sunday 8am, 10am,
Weekday
8am, 9am, 12:10pm
Holyday
Vigil Mass
8am, 9am,

INTRODUCTION

CONGRATULATIONS! IF YOU HAVE picked up this book, there's a good chance that you've just gotten engaged (or may be soon!) and are embarking on your wedding planning journey. You likely have some idea of what you would like to wear on the big day (and maybe even to some of the events leading up to it), but like most brides-to-be, you aren't completely sure yet. You're probably feeling a mix of emotions—ranging from excitement to overwhelm—and perhaps you're even a little scared.

Let me assure you that all of this is totally normal.

It's no secret that planning a wedding is stressful. Yet few people talk about what a huge undertaking it is to plan just the fashion-related aspects! While Hollywood scriptwriters and curated Instagram galleries will have you believe that shopping for your dress is a magical, flawless experience full of bubbles and fun, the reality is usually far more complicated. *Yes*, dress shopping *can* be exciting, but it can also be daunting, frustrating, and even *humiliating* when you don't know where to look, what to expect, or how to prepare yourself for the inevitable challenges in the fitting room.

Add in the fact that most couples have an average of *four* wedding-related events (with some having as many as ten!) that all require different outfits, and things become more complicated. So, if you're not feeling 24/7 thrills, please know that it's not just you. It's the way the system and industry have been set up. Thanks to a lack of transparency and inclusion, most brides end up feeling a bit disillusioned and confused during the process. This is not helped by the fact that, as a society, we place enormous pressure on brides to look "perfect" on their wedding day. There isn't a safe space to share the many struggles they go through in an attempt to live up to expectations on what is often the biggest fashion moment of their lives. It is easy to end up in the middle of a perfect storm, feeling isolated and anxious during what should be one of the happiest times of their lives.

I get it because I have been there.

When I got engaged back in 2000, the wedding industry (and the world) was nothing like it is now. I was working in finance, and wedding fashion was still relatively niche. Information was limited to a few monthly magazines and even *fewer* books on the subject. Designers had minimalistic, uninformative websites (if they had one at all), and there were no social media galleries to help you get a sense of what was out there. Inspiration came by way of celebrity dresses that were often custom-made or far beyond the average bride's price point. If you didn't find what you were looking for in the current issue of *Brides* or the random book with outdated fashions, it was pretty much tough luck until the next one was published.

It also didn't help that, at age twenty-four, none of my friends had planned a wedding, so I didn't have any peers to turn to for advice on where to look and what to look for. Still, I had watched all the movies, so I assumed that trying on dresses and finding *the one* was going to be a dreamy Cinderella moment. I made my first appointment at Vera Wang on Madison Avenue and planned for a wonderful experience where I would walk in, be handed champagne, try on three to five dresses, and then have that *aha* moment where we all gasp, knowing I had found the one. After all, you just "know," right? *Wrong*.

While the staff couldn't have been nicer and the dresses more gorgeous, I quickly realized that I had no idea what I wanted and this wasn't going to be at all what it is like in the movies. I was crushed. I wound up spending months trying on hundreds of dresses on lunch breaks, after work, and on weekends, feeling more and more confused about what to look for and why what I thought I wanted didn't look right on me at all. I had a real crisis of confidence that left me feeling alone and confused about what was supposed to be the happiest time of my life. I looked for someone to guide me through the process, desperately wishing that someone could understand me, my body type, wedding style, and personal preferences and just tell me where to go. It seemed like there had to be someone out there who knew the market and could help. But my searches came up empty, and I was on my own.

Eventually I found a dress that I loved and realized that it was only the beginning. What were my bridesmaids going to wear? Or my fiancé? Or my mom? I found myself wishing for help over and over again that year. Despite how tough this was for me, it also planted a seed for what would become my career. Since then, I have made it my mission to help brides avoid the stress and struggle I faced. I do this not by simply helping them find their dream gown but by also guiding them through a personal journey to help them identify their style, highlight what they love, camouflage things they don't, and ignite that inner glow that helps them look and, more importantly, *feel* beautiful.

Since founding my company, The Stylish Bride®, in 2004 I have supported thousands of clients on their journey to find their perfect dress. This is something I am deeply proud of, and to this day, for me, there is nothing better than when my clients feel confident, comfortable, and beautiful. However, the end product doesn't come without a significant amount of work, and for those who don't have help, it can be quite a challenge. While a majority of women admit to fantasizing about their wedding day and dress, most have an incomplete notion of what they actually want to wear but feel it needs to be "perfect." To complicate matters further, the vast majority of us also have body shapes that don't fit the "runway ideal"—size 4, which is who the bridal salon samples are made to fit—and are equipped with little to no real understanding of how to navigate the antiquated and often exhausting journey of shopping for a wedding dress. Add on the numerous psychological hurdles one feels when planning a wedding, and it's clear why so many brides admit to being disappointed with their shopping experience—or worse, their dress.

Throughout my career, I have seen it all and learned how to navigate just about every fashion-related issue there is. I have comforted brides as they broke down in dressing rooms, unable to zip up the sample dress, and then witnessed firsthand the joy they feel when I bust out a few simple tools to help make the dress fit after all (more on the product I developed to fix this later). I also know how much a great wedding wardrobe impacts a bride's overall experience—and memory—of her wedding; I've listened to women (who weren't my clients) talk about buying a dress that "looked great" but that they felt awkward wearing. I've had other brides tell me how glad they were that they went with their gut and chose the dress their sister swore was a mistake. And I know how to curate and create a shopping experience that saves time, money, and sanity.

My experiences have equipped me with a unique skill set that I will share in this book. It is my goal to set you up for success from the very start, helping you to plan for obstacles before they arrive and arming you with the knowledge you need to find what you don't even know you're looking for—in a way that is seamless and fun.

Now, instead of scrolling through Instagram, growing increasingly frazzled by thousands of images, you will be shown how to quiet the noise, tap into your own unique style, and wisely use social media to your advantage. I'll share insider tips on choosing which boutiques to visit, working successfully with consultants, making sample sizes fit, and avoiding a whole host of costly mistakes right from the start. I'll also offer meaningful ways to mitigate potential family drama, comprehensive strategies for dressing the entire bridal party, and proven, practical solutions for the trickiest of dilemmas that can arise around a wedding. You're also going to learn some timeless styling tricks that will support you in looking and feeling your best long after your wedding day.

I hope you will find this to be an inclusive self-love manifesto written to educate, empower, and empathize with you, regardless of your size, shape, age, or background. I have worked hard to pack the book with useful information, stunning visuals, expert advice, and timeless tips, all in an attempt to help you silence the noise, zone in on your own unique style, and emerge with an authentic air of confidence and self-acceptance that will help you shine your brightest on your wedding day and well into your marriage.

I can't wait to go on this journey with you!

Chapter 1

A FEW THINGS BEFORE WE BEGIN

AS WE BEGIN THIS journey together, I'd like to start by sharing what you should—*and shouldn't*—expect in the pages ahead. First and foremost, do not expect me to simply tell you what to wear or what is beautiful. While this might seem like the easiest thing for both of us, it's completely against everything I stand for personally and professionally. I firmly believe that style is an expression of who you are and where you are in your life; therefore, *you* are the only one who can decide what is truly best for you and what makes you feel confident and beautiful. As such, simply giving you a list of trends and fail-proof "classic" options and calling it a day is not only a total waste of your time, but it would not honor everything that makes you special.

Instead, think of me as your guide. I am going to equip you with key information, just as I do with my individual styling clients, to empower, inform, and support you as you do the work to create a wedding wardrobe that makes you feel beautiful and expresses all that you are in a way that is utterly timeless.

This process will be fun, insightful, and authentic—*but it won't be easy*. You will be challenged to take a deep dive into your ideas about yourself, your boundaries, your beliefs, and the ways you present yourself to the world. If there is one thing I have learned in my two decades in this business, it is that weddings are wonderfully exciting, but they are also rich with feelings, opinions, pressure, and triggers—and the bride is often right at the center of it all.

This is why trusting yourself is so important, even if it's the hardest part of defining ourselves. As humans, we are hardwired to want to fit in, which makes it hard to shut out the noise and do what feels right to us. It often feels as though we're downright encouraged to live in a state of self-doubt. Whether it's magazine editors telling us our favorite looks are "out," advertisements making us feel that our noses/breasts/butts need to be a certain size to be beautiful, or people in our inner circle critiquing the things we love, listening to ourselves can feel like a terrifying act of rebellion.

I realize that truly listening to yourself is easier said than done. I struggle with it every day myself. But to really get the full benefit of this book, you must try—and I will help you along the way. While I am here to offer advice and guidance, at the end of the day your wedding day is about honoring the commitment of marriage. It will only feel right if everything authentically represents your unique personality and preferences, and only you can uncover what they are, and I will show you how. You will hear me talk a lot about feeling beautiful in this book. This is because I truly believe that comfort equals confidence. I don't mean one should not suffer a tiny bit for fashion—I am reminded of this every time I wear my Spanx—but feeling constricted or uncomfortable is a one-way ticket to regret.

With this in mind, I want you to make yourself a promise right here: From this moment on, you will listen to suggestions and keep an open mind, but at the end of the day, you will retain all veto power and you will only say "yes" when it feels completely right for you.

Deal?

Great! Let's get started.

YOU ARE BEAUTIFUL AS YOU ARE *RIGHT NOW.*

Take this to heart and remind yourself of it every single day (multiple times, if necessary). Becoming engaged is such an exciting time, but it can also be stressful for those who don't enjoy the spotlight or have body insecurities that leave them feeling badly about themselves. When those thoughts creep in, remember your partner has chosen to live the rest of their life with you *as you are right now*.

You may want to make your skin glow a bit more, lose a little weight, or tone up, and that's all fine—do what you feel is best for you. But please do not allow external influences to make you feel less than you are. The idea that you have to achieve some limited idea of perfection to be a beautiful bride is harmful to your self-worth, and you deserve more. This will never be truer than when shopping for a wedding dress, which can exacerbate insecurities.

As lovely as the dress-shopping process can be, the reality is that you will be dealing with an antiquated and *deeply flawed* sizing system and a fashion industry that doesn't suit much of the population, as I'll explain in chapter 4. For now, embrace the reality that you are beautiful and worthy of every happiness—whatever your shape and size.

STYLE IS A SCIENCE, NOT A GIFT.

If you have ever looked at photos of Amal Clooney, Jackie Kennedy, Grace Kelly, Olivia Palermo—or anyone else—and wished you had their "easy, effortless style," you're not alone. Just as we have been brainwashed to believe that real skin doesn't have pores, wrinkles, or blemishes and most bodies don't have cellulite and wiggly bits, there is a false belief that when it comes to style, you've either got it or you don't. This is a myth the fashion industry loves to perpetuate because it widens the gap between the average Jane and the fashion icons on magazine covers and fills it with that mysterious X factor no one really has and everyone wants. Like everything else, dressing well is a science and it takes practice. Best of all, it's something everyone can learn.

The important thing to remember when you're looking at Amal, Jackie, Grace, Olivia, and *every other celebrity you admire* is that most of them have (or have had) a trained stylist behind the scenes making sure they look picture-perfect. Yes, some people have an innate passion and talent for mixing textures and colors and creating looks, but even then, it takes practice. The point? It's normal to be intimidated by fashion (again, the game is set up that way), but like most things in life, it's just a series of steps. Once you get the basics down and do the work to understand who you are and what you like, dressing well becomes a wonderful, fun, and exhilarating experience.

IDENTIFYING YOUR PERSONAL STYLE IS A PROCESS OF DISCOVERY.

To help you find the dress of your dreams and create a wedding wardrobe you love, we will start by identifying your current core style. I say *current* because your core style isn't fixed; it changes as you change, grows as you grow, and expands as you are exposed to new information and possibilities.

As you read through this book, I want you to allow yourself the space to sit in the discomfort of not knowing what you want. We live in a world that demands instant gratification and perpetuates the idea that not having an immediate "hell yes" means it's a "hell no." To me this seems so limiting because it smothers the chance for expansion and growth. There's something to be said for enjoying the journey in life and shopping. I like to think of it the same way one would enjoy a lovely tasting menu or listen to a friend's playlist. Some things may be unfamiliar, but that doesn't necessarily make them wrong for you.

Likewise with choosing a wedding dress style: Give yourself time to sit with fresh ideas and looks, revisit them over a few different days, and make sure you get a real sense of what you think before you take something off your list of possibilities. Alternatively, even if you love something, give yourself a day or two and revisit it to make sure you still love it—and perhaps avoid a costly mistake.

YOU MIGHT FEEL A LITTLE OVERWHELMED AT FIRST—*AND THAT'S OK.*

The information in this book may feel a little overwhelming at times—I get it! It's completely normal to freeze when presented with all of the things you didn't know you didn't know. But again, everything in this book has been carefully designed to equip you with the tools you need to make the shopping process as seamless and effective as possible. For example, instead of looking at the lists of fabrics and shapes and feeling overwhelmed, remember this is just information to be used as a quick reference to help you find the key pieces that work for you.

BRINING LUXURY TO REALITY

I'd also like to address the fact that I've spent my career working on weddings that fall into the "luxury" category. While that is my background and what you will often see reflected on these pages, I know this isn't the reality for most brides, and I'm by no means suggesting that it should be. However, if you strip away the designer names and the big budgets, I believe the core principle is the same: Every woman deserves to look and feel beautiful on their wedding day. For me, not only is this a "nice to have," it's essential. As such, my team and I have spent the last few years translating our knowledge into free resources on our website in an effort to support as many brides as we can. These guides, downloads, and other forms of media will be helpful no matter what the budget. We have also included loads of supplemental content that supports this book and can be accessed by scanning the QR code at the end of every chapter. If you see or read something in this book that seems over-the-top or unattainable, it probably is, but I'm including it because there is something that can be learned from it.

WE BELIEVE LOVE IS LOVE.

At The Stylish Bride® we believe the only thing that matters is love. We celebrate *every* type of person and couple out there and feel honored to be a resource for them. Throughout this book, we reference the *bride* and *groom* frequently, but that doesn't mean we have only one view of marriage. At times I will discuss how a topic pertains to two brides or two grooms. I embrace diversity and aim to present my ideas in such a way that everyone feels included.

HOW THIS BOOK IS ORGANIZED

Throughout the course of your wedding planning journey, you will be faced with an astounding number of decisions, and the order in which you make them is more important than you may anticipate. For example, going wedding dress shopping before you know the details of your location and venue can prove to be a costly mistake. And did you know that your mom should select her dress *after* you know what the bridesmaids will be wearing? All of these little nuances are virtually unknown to a bride, yet so important.

While there are a lot of articles online to answer questions and guide brides through the process, I have never found one that includes timeline information beyond basic tips for wedding dress shopping, and most brides are faced with more than forty fashion decisions (if not more!) they need to make.

The lack of information on when to do each piece blows my mind because just as wedding planning has a process, there is a structure to styling and putting a wedding fashion story together—and it begins with *you*.

At The Stylish Bride®, the foundation of our work is understanding what makes our clients feel comfortable, confident, and beautiful and then guiding them as they build a wedding wardrobe they love. I am going to do the same for you in this book.

Just as fashion elements build on each other and each decision affects another, I've organized the content of this book to coincide with the suggested timeline that we use with our clients.

Whether you choose to read it straight through or flip to the section you need, you will stay on course. I have included QR codes at the end of each chapter, which lead to lots of supplemental downloads, checklists, and guides on our website. I encourage you to use all of the resources my team and I have created for you and keep visiting our website for updated information.

REMEMBER TO HAVE FUN!

What I want most is for you to feel comfortable, confident, and beautiful on your wedding day and every day, but I also want this to be FUN for you. This book was written to remove a lot of the stress and confusion that often steals the joy from shopping for a wedding dress and other wedding-related pieces. I hope that the content, tips, fun facts, and exercises that are presented help you enjoy the process. My team and I are always accessible through my website at www.TheStylishBride.com if you need anything. We would love to hear from you, see the dress you chose, or even help you through our in-person or virtual styling program.

Before we get started with your Blueprint in the next chapter, the following pages provide a timeline of what to work on and when.

TIMELINE FOR WEDDING DRESS PREP

In my line of business, planning is *everything*. Knowing exactly what to do and when to do it is not only essential when working with clients, but it also allows you to be ahead of the game when sourcing items from vendors who are all juggling dozens of other clients and responsibilities.

While we have seen engagements last between six months and two years, the average time for our clients is 14 months, which is what we will be using for the purpose of this book. If you are on a shorter or longer timeline, don't worry! You can simply adjust the items below to fit your needs. Here's everything you will need to do.

14 MONTHS: SET THE DETAILS

I dare say this is the most important part of your wedding-planning process, as the details play such a large role in the selection of your dress. Don't even think of shopping for a dress until you have this information.

- ☐ Lock in your wedding date.
- ☐ Set the dress code.
- ☐ Do the **Bridal Style Blueprint** (**on page 32**) to identify your personal style and how to translate that to wedding style.

13 MONTHS: MAKE A PLAN

Because a well-thought-out wedding dress shopping plan takes time and careful consideration to put together, this month is all about strategy and setting the tone for a stress-free shopping experience.

- ☐ Identify the stores in your area that carry the designers you are interested in.
- ☐ Book your appointments in a strategic order so that you can maximize the experience.
- ☐ Decide who to bring shopping with you (no more than two people).
- ☐ Order/gather all items you need to bring to make shopping easier.

12 MONTHS: TIME TO SHOP

This is the month your hard work and preparation pays off, and you get to start trying on dresses—enjoy!

- ☐ Print out your Style Summary and bring it with you.
- ☐ Start a shared album for photos/videos and designate one of your people to be the photographer for a day.
- ☐ Download a photo collage app to use for comparing dresses while shopping.

11 MONTHS: DRESS DECISION TIME

At this point, you've gone to several stores and tried on many gorgeous dresses, and it's time to make a decision. Take your time, follow the plan, and remember my rule of thumb: **doubt means *don't*!**

- ☐ Revisit boutiques if needed.
- ☐ Do our Shine Test to find out if the dress is THE one.
- ☐ On the purchase contract, make sure they note any customizations or changes that will be made to the dress during production of the dress.
- ☐ When you are ready, place your wedding gown order (remember, you are putting down a 50 percent non-refundable deposit).
- ☐ Confirm the due date with the store so you can follow up on progress as the due date approaches.
- ☐ Ask when you should call to book your first fitting, and mark it on your calendar.

10 MONTHS: ENGAGEMENT PHOTOS

Engagement photos can happen at many different times in the process, but we find that the 10-month mark is generally a great time to do them. You will not only have them for your wedding website, but you will have worked with your photographer and will feel more confident in front of the camera.

- ☐ Schedule a date and location for the shoot with your photographer.
- ☐ Use this as an opportunity to try out a hair and makeup team.
- ☐ Consider how many looks you are going to do on the shoot (up to three) and what you own that will work for each.
- ☐ Coordinate your partner's outfit(s).
- ☐ Organize and steam all items so they are ready to go on shoot day.
- ☐ Hire a stylist to help you during the shoot.

9 MONTHS: BRIDESMAID DRESS CONCEPT

Selecting bridesmaid dresses is arguably one of the hardest parts of being a bride and often the thing that brides struggle with the most, so we like to start on them early. One quick note: You must have decided on your wedding dress before beginning this selection because you need to know what your dress is going to look like, as it will influence the choice for bridesmaid dresses.

- ☐ Determine the ideal color palette for your bridesmaid dresses. Place your choices side-by-side with the wedding dress to see how they look.
- ☐ Decide who is paying for the dress—you or the bridesmaids.
- ☐ Look on Instagram and Pinterest for inspiration.
- ☐ Decide which of these looks you want to have:
  - ☐ Matching: Everyone wears the same dress in the same color.
  - ☐ Coordinating: Not all dresses are the same, but they are all part of the same collection or color palette.
  - ☐ Mix and Match: None of the dresses are the same, and the coordinating detail is a color or pattern.

8 MONTHS: BRIDESMAID DRESS ORDER

Just like your wedding dress, many bridesmaid dresses require you to place an order and have the dresses made for you. This process can take several months (general timeline is 16 weeks), and you will want to give your ladies plenty of time for alterations, because chances are, they will really need it.

- ☐ Have all bridesmaids select the dress they want (if you are giving them options).
- ☐ Have their measurements taken.
- ☐ Place the order with the dress company you are using, or purchase the individual dresses they will be wearing.

7 MONTHS: OTHER OUTFITS FOR THE BRIDE

You are most likely going to need a few outfits for your wedding weekend, and it's a good idea to get started on them now.

- ☐ Decide if you want to wear white at every event or mix it up.
- ☐ Go back to your Bridal Style Blueprint and start thinking about applying your style profile to the looks you need to select.
- ☐ Create an Attire Board for each event.

Also:

- ☐ This is the time to book your Wedding Day Dresser so that you can ensure you have the help you need on your wedding day.

6 MONTHS: MOMS

Moms often have the hardest time of anyone finding a dress they love. There are just so many facets to dressing appropriately for the occasion and feeling confident, comfortable, and beautiful. It's a good idea to get started well in advance.

- ☐ Have the mothers of the bride and groom both do the Bridal Style Blueprint to get a sense of what they like wearing.
- ☐ Share with them the color palette of the wedding and any important notes/preferences that will impact their sartorial choices.
- ☐ Create an Attire Board for each mom.
- ☐ Home in on dress shape and details.
- ☐ Understand the options for adding arm coverage, if needed or desired.

5 MONTHS: MEN & CHILDREN

At this point, you need to start thinking about what your groom and groomsmen will wear and order their outfits and accessories. It's also the time to select attire for any children in your wedding party. You don't want to get children's clothing or shoes too early because they will grow, but you also want to give yourself time to find them something you love.

Men

- ☐ Decide whether men will be buying or renting suits/tuxedos.
- ☐ Choose the overall looks for attire.
- ☐ Arrange fittings.

Children

- ☐ Come up with a concept: traditional, whimsical, or modern.
- ☐ Choose comfortable shoes. I've helped many tiny feet in my day, and it's so sad when they are crying (and sometimes refusing to wear the shoe entirely!).
- ☐ Coordinate with their parents on their sizes and estimate what size they will be at the time of the wedding.

4 MONTHS: ACCESSORIES

You may have been thinking about this and choosing pieces along the way, but if not, now is the time. Your wedding dress fittings will start soon (about two months before the wedding), and you will want options to try on with your dress.

- ☐ Choose your shoes (you will need these for your first fitting).
- ☐ Choose jewelry options (if undecided, bring them to your second fitting).
- ☐ Choose your "something old, new, borrowed, and blue."
- ☐ If you plan to rent jewelry, this is the time to start considering different pieces.

3 MONTHS: UNDERGARMENTS, ROBES, AND GIFTS

At this point in the process, things are starting to heat up. You have lots of decisions to make and details to take care of—deep breaths! In terms of the fashion, you are going to want to order undergarment options to have for your first fitting, purchase getting-ready robes (or dresses, PJs, or shirts) for you and your bridesmaids, and decide what you are gifting the members of your wedding party.

- ☐ Purchase several undergarment options for each needed piece (shapewear, bust support, etc.) so you can choose the ones that best suit your dress at the fitting.
- ☐ Choose your getting-ready outfit (nothing you have to pull over your head).
- ☐ Coordinate getting-ready outfits for your bridal party and purchase them, if you plan to do this.
- ☐ Select gifts for the bridal party. For bridesmaids, earrings and small jewelry make a great gift and can be worn by the party to ensure consistency in the overall look.
- ☐ Similarly, the groom might consider bow ties, shirt studs, and cufflinks for his groomsmen, which is a nice way to give them a gift while also ensuring that everyone looks the same when standing together as a group.

2 MONTHS: FITTINGS

Wedding dress fittings start now, and you are going to want to be prepared. There are several things you need to think about.

- ☐ Don't forget your shoes for the fittings! If you do (and trust me, it happens a lot!) they won't be able to work on the length, which is a huge part of the process.
- ☐ This is the deadline for any fitness goals so you are where you want to be when the fittings start.
- ☐ Decide whether you want to pick up or ship your wedding dress.
- ☐ Bring all of your jewelry and accessories to the second wedding dress fitting to see how they look together.
- ☐ At your final fitting, take a video of how to bustle your dress and share it with the person who will be doing it.

Also:

- ☐ Check in with your bridesmaids to make sure their dresses have arrived, they've tried them on, and then schedule alterations as needed.
- ☐ Do the same for the children's clothes.

1 MONTH: FINAL DETAILS

It's all coming together, and you're getting close! Here is what you need to be thinking about so that you're white-carpet ready.

- ☐ This is the moment to create a good packing checklist, so you don't forget anything!
- ☐ Start to pack for the wedding weekend by putting all attire items in their own area.
- ☐ Group outfits together and label them.
- ☐ Purchase your Fashion Emergency Kit.
- ☐ Purchase extra nude undies, shapewear, bust-lift tape, socks, blister-block, etc. to have on hand.
- ☐ Create a plan for where you will hang your dress at the venue.
- ☐ If you don't have a professional dresser coming that day, purchase a quality handheld or full-size garment steamer and watch videos on how to do it properly. (I really don't recommend this route, but if you can't hire a dresser, it's better than a wrinkled dress.)

- ☐ Pack a separate suitcase for the honeymoon, if applicable.
- ☐ Make sure all bridesmaids have had their fittings and are set with their dresses and accessories.
- ☐ Final fitting takes place for the wedding dress and all other items.

1 WEEK TO GO: ON-SITE PREPARATION

When you arrive at the place where you will get ready on your wedding day, you will want to take care of your dress properly so that nothing happens to it.

- ☐ Hang up your dress in a place that is out of the way, and high, so that the bag isn't lying on the floor.
- ☐ If you are arriving at a destination venue or hotel, ask for a rolling garment rack to be put in your room. Unpack upon arrival and keep items grouped together.

THE WEDDING DAY!

It's here!!! Congratulations! A few tips for making the most of it.

- ☐ Give yourself plenty of time to get dressed so you are not rushed.
- ☐ Make sure your mother and any other important people who will be helping you are already dressed for the day, so that they look good in photos.
- ☐ Have your Fashion Emergency Kit on hand in case something goes wrong. Remember, at every wedding something goes wrong, but how you react to it is up to you. Take a deep breath (or five!) and roll with it. Sometimes those mishaps are the best stories afterwards!

1 MONTH AFTER: WHAT TO DO WITH YOUR DRESS

- ☐ Decide whether you want to clean and preserve your dress, donate it, sell it, or repurpose it.

Chapter 2

BLUEPRINT FOR WEDDING DRESS SUCCESS

LET'S HAVE SOME FUN and start with a question: How do you feel about what you are wearing right now? What is the shirt/dress/jumpsuit you're wearing telling the world about you? How accurate is the message? In full disclosure, I'm sitting here in yoga pants and a cashmere hoodie as I type this, so this question isn't to shame you; it's to get at something important: the difference between style and fashion. So if you are like me and cozy in your loungewear, do this mental exercise by thinking of what you wore the last time you got dressed to go out and loved your outfit. Hold on to that image because you will need it shortly.

DISCOVERING YOUR CORE STYLE

When people talk about style, most people think about clothes, but that's fashion. *Style* is something different. It's expressive, energetic, and *deeply personal*. I like to think of it as the outward expression of who you are at your core—a gorgeous mixture of your values, beliefs, likes, dislikes, and creativity. Understanding your style is so much more than knowing that you like Amal Clooney's pantsuits and Grace Kelly's wedding dress. It's knowing what feels authentic to you on a cellular level—your sartorial intuition, if you will.

Your sense of style is what will make the wrong clothes feel restrictive and bring the right clothes to life. It's important to note that, like other areas of your life, it will evolve throughout the years. Just as you grow and develop, so do your fashion choices; so don't be surprised if you once loved neutrals and suddenly find yourself leaning into brighter hues or if you suddenly feel less enthusiastic about trendier cuts and start swooning over traditional A-lines. None of this means anything more than that you have changed—and that's a good thing!

Still, figuring out one's core style can be difficult for even the most self-aware bride. And if you're like most people who have a closet full of clothes they no longer wear or have *never* worn, with a bunch of autopilot purchases wedged in between (cough: five pairs of black trousers), it can feel downright overwhelming. But knowing what you love on others versus what you love on *yourself* is the most important step in the shopping process, so get ready.

In this chapter, I am going to show you how to identify and lean into your personal style, which will not only help you to find the wedding dress of your dreams but also create a wedding wardrobe that feels like a second skin and looks fresh and beautiful.

CREATING YOUR BRIDAL STYLE BLUEPRINT

One's wedding day has long been considered the most important fashion moment in a woman's life, but today's bride is under more pressure than ever before to get it right. Not only is she expected to look incredible, but to do so in a way that's unique and *totally authentic to her*. That's a tall order for any bride, but if you're someone who likes a lot of different looks, it's easy to feel a bit lost.

Over the years, I've perfected a process to help my clients get to the heart of their style and pinpoint what they want before they start visiting stores or going on a social media doom scroll. By digging deep and asking the right questions up-front, I've helped thousands of women save time and money, reduce stress, and most importantly, find a dress they love.

In this section, I am going to show you how to use my **Bridal Style Blueprint**, which you can find on page 32, to help you identify your core style and seamlessly translate it into a wedding dress style. This will not only provide insight into your everyday wardrobe but also ensure that you have a strong sense of what kind of dress you are looking for before you ever step foot into a bridal salon. By the time you're finished with this section, you're going to have all the information you need in one place, which will allow you to select the designers you want to see and make a targeted shopping plan. The goal is to not only give you a better sense of who you are style-wise but also help you understand how that translates to your wedding style. Let's get started!

There are six main sections to the Bridal Style Blueprint:

1. The details of the wedding
2. Your Personal Style Cocktail
3. Dress elements you love
4. Body type
5. Dress shape
6. Budget

This tool is the exact summary I give to each store consultant when my clients and I begin a dress appointment. It tells them everything they need to know to help them find a dress our bride will love.

Let's dive in!

1. Details of the Wedding

Your wedding dress needs to be in harmony with your surroundings. To do this, we must consider the details of the wedding.

- **Date/weather:** Consider the season and how that will affect your dress choice.
- **Time of day:** If it's an afternoon wedding, your dress may have a different feel than one for an evening wedding.
- **Venue:** Perhaps the most important of all of these details is where you have the ceremony and reception.
- **Formality of the event:** What type of attire are you suggesting on the invitation? You should always be in line, or slightly more formal, than what your guests are wearing.

So now think about your own wedding and what your details are.

2. Your Personal Style Cocktail

I like the concept of the "Style Cocktail" because it so clearly illustrates how a few key ingredients combine to make a fantastic whole. Think of it like your favorite cocktail: You have a core spirit, a supporting mixer, and a garnish to give it a pop of flavor.

For example, I would say that my **Style Cocktail** is classic and feminine with a pop of sparkle. I actually think of my Style Cocktail all the time—I use it when I'm deciding what to wear in lots of different situations and when I'm shopping and trying to decide if I should buy something. These words are important because we will use them in a later section to narrow down the designers that are a good fit for you. They can also steer a store's dress consultant toward what you are looking for.

Take a peek into your closet.

To identify your particular mix, let's start by heading to your closet and looking for details that repeat themselves. Are there a lot of sequins or bows? Do you gravitate toward a certain silhouette, like A-lines or straight skirts? If you really *look*, you will notice the trends that emerge, in both shape and detail.

As you peruse what you have, I want you to do a little tally next to each detail category on the Blueprint worksheet included in this chapter (page 32). Ultimately, you are going to

Quick Guide to Dress Codes

As the host of the wedding, it's your job to set a dress code that makes your guests feel comfortable and to communicate it effectively. That means not getting too creative with the wording and staying away from terms like "California Black Tie" or "Gatsby Cocktail" that people won't understand. With that said, here are five main attire levels we use in the United States:

1. **Black tie:** This is the most common choice for couples who want a bit of red-carpet magic on their big day. This means a tuxedo with a white French cuffed shirt (worn with elegant cufflinks) for men. Women are to wear full-length dresses (you may be able to get away with tea-length, but anything shorter is a no-no), and the dresses should not be too revealing. Very formal trousers or suits for women are also acceptable.
2. **Formal:** A classic dark suit for men, and elegant cocktail dresses, beautiful pantsuits, or longer-length gowns for women. Should you choose to dress your wedding party in formal attire, my advice is (again) to keep it consistent. All the women should be in the same length of dress and the men should be in matching suits. While there are some lovely photos on Pinterest of coordinating suits in various colors, this is incredibly hard to do and can look bad *fast*. So, when outfitting your wedding party in suits, my advice is to keep it cohesive and add interest with accessories.
3. **Cocktail:** This is a jazzier version of formal and allows you a bit more room to have fun with your outfits. Men should be wearing a suit jacket or blazer, but it doesn't necessarily have to be a suit and can be in a more interesting fabric. In warmer weather, you want to focus on lighter fabrics and colors. Women can wear less formal tea-length dresses with fun details, but stay away from fully beaded gowns or things that skew highly formal.
4. **Semiformal:** Less formal than cocktail attire, but as with cocktail attire, men should wear a jacket (tie not required) and aim to look fresh and put together. Women can wear short or long dresses with flirty details and bolder prints or florals. The dress code for a nice garden party or Sunday best might be a good way to think about it.
5. **Casual:** Designer Tom Ford famously said, "Dressing well is a form of good manners," and this quote is a great guide for a casual invitation. While often used for day events, I think the British concept of "smart casual" works well here—more stylish than business attire and more elegant than formal. Beautiful dresses and pantsuits with fantastic accessories for women and long-sleeved button-down shirts, blazers, and dress pants for men. Khakis are acceptable as long as they fit you properly and look polished. No to these items: T-shirts, jeans/denim, sneakers, shorts, or anything too revealing for women.

check the boxes next to the top three. Then, you'll have a better understanding of your own recipe. You might start to realize you're a chic Manhattan who loves sleek styles *à la* Angelina Jolie in *Mr. and Mrs. Smith*, or perhaps you're a French martini who loves to mix sex appeal and feminine glamour, like Penelope Cruz. (See the stunning pink Versace dress she wore to the Oscars in 2007.) Perhaps you're a classic and clean vodka soda with a splash of lime who loves anything and everything worn by Grace Kelly. The point is to know what your elements are and play with them like a fashion mixologist.

I can hear you saying, "That all sounds great, Julie, but I am not just one thing—how boring!" And you're absolutely right! Just like the women who wear the clothes, personal style is rarely one-dimensional. We are multifaceted human beings with wonderfully different sides of ourselves! Let me explain: Having a core style doesn't mean you lack imagination; it just means that you know what shapes, details, fabrics, and accessories make you look and feel great, and you use that knowledge to your advantage. Even more importantly, you know what you don't like and should steer clear of—a massive time- and money-saving hack if there ever was one. The great news is that once you know what your elements are, a new chapter in your life begins, and it will serve as a guide long after you find your wedding dress.

Another way I get to the bottom of what my clients really like to wear is by asking them about their favorite outfits in different settings.

Here are examples of the questions, and how I would answer them by looking at my closet.

1. What do you like to wear when you go out to dinner on a Saturday night in the winter and summer? (Do both if you live in a place where there are seasons.)
   - *When I am going out to dinner at night in the winter, I typically wear black jeans or pants with a nice black top and a sparkly necklace.*
   - *In the summer, I'm much more inclined to wear color—dresses or a skirt-and-top combination.*
2. What do you wear to an important meeting or interview?
   - *When I have a new client meeting, I pull out my favorite skirt with a feminine sweater and a colorful scarf.*
3. What is your go-to dress when going to a black-tie affair or to someone else's wedding?
   - *I feel like you can never go wrong with a strapless A-line gown in a great fabric with a statement necklace.*

3. Dress Elements You Love

What kind of clothing details do you gravitate toward? For example, do you have a few sequin dresses in your closet? How about lace? While most women don't wear these things every day, the way you dress for a special occasion is a great indicator of the details you like.

- **Embellishments:** When you look at your wardrobe, are you seeing feathers, sequins, sparkles, or lace? Or none of the above and you prefer a great simple cut?
- **Fabrics:** I'm always interested in what my clients gravitate toward the most. Do they like stiff fabrics that have more structure? Or soft and silky fabrics? When you start wedding dress shopping, you will want to understand which fabrics you tend to like most.

4. Body Type

Every woman I've ever met has been intimately acquainted with what she perceives as her physical flaws and her body type. And while there is a reality to what your shape is, I guarantee that you are your own worst critic. Therefore, we always start by asking our clients what they like to accentuate, and then we get to what they like to minimize.

Understanding what works best on your body and the shapes you are most comfortable wearing is a *critical* piece of the puzzle, but not always a simple one to tease out. This is because, like everything in style, it's *subjective*. There is no right or wrong, only what makes you *feel* good. For example, the suggestion that a pear-shaped bride shouldn't wear a trumpet- or mermaid-style dress may be wrong for you because you like showing your curves. If that's the case, then you should!

But if you are anything like me, you are probably looking for guidance on how to apply the realities of your shape and your preferences when you shop for your wedding dress. I remember thinking often to myself, "Can't someone just tell me what will look good on me?"

The short answer is *yes*—and *no*.

When it comes to discussing body types, I'm not a huge fan of the fruit comparisons—apple, pear, banana, strawberry, etc.—but I've searched and not yet found a better way to illustrate this! So here is a guide to the five main body types.

BODY TYPE

Busty

Apple

Rectangle

Hourglass

Pear

5. Dress Shape

Now let's consider the different wedding dress shape options.

Here is a general guideline on the dress styles that flatter different body shapes (see Chapter 3 for more details on the types of dress silhouettes, necklines, and sleeves):

Body Part	Styles That Accentuate	Styles That Minimize
Shoulders	Portrait, off-the-shoulder, and high necklines	Strapless, sleeveless (has a strap), any length sleeves
Bust	V-necks, sweethearts	Straight-across necklines, ruching, fold-over detail
Back	Open back	Anything with coverage
Arms	High neck, sleeveless, strapless	Portrait/off-the-shoulder necklines, sleeves
Waist	Anything that is nipped in at your narrowest part	Shifts and ruched fabrics
Tush	Trumpet and mermaid skirts	A-lines and ball gowns
Thighs	Trumpet and mermaid skirts	A-lines and ball gowns

It can also be really helpful to look in your closet again and notice the clothing shapes that you gravitate toward. For example, I love a V-neck shirt and an A-line skirt because I personally feel the best when I accentuate my waist and minimize my hips. Over and over, I see this in the shapes of clothing I choose.

One quick note: Because bridal shapes can be different from what you find in your closet (I mean, let's face it—not too many women own a ball gown these days), you should plan on trying several different styles just to make sure. Plus, sometimes knowing what you *don't* want is just as important as knowing what you *do* want!

Merging the two: As the illustration on the following page shows, there are tried-and-true clothing shapes that work on every body type. Because most women feel the best when they think their body shape is shown to its best advantage, I encourage you to try on the recommended clothing shape for your figure. Still, it's entirely possible that you will prefer something else, so it's good to explore several options.

BODY TYPE & DRESS SHAPE

Pear
Ball Gown
A-Line
Princess
Busty
Trumpet
A-Line
Mermaid
Hourglass
Trumpet
Princess
Sheath

6. Budget

Most often, when I ask my clients what price point they are comfortable with, they have absolutely no idea what wedding dresses cost. I'm not surprised, because the wedding industry is frustratingly opaque about their prices. That can make it hard to decide what your price range is and stay within it.

We will dive into setting a budget and what you get for your money at every price range in chapter 5, so for now, just start to think of what you are comfortable with. To give you an idea, the national average that brides in the United States spend on their wedding dresses is $2,400 and varies greatly by location. For our purposes, I define a designer wedding dress as one that is over $4,000, which is the entry price point you will see at most high-end salons.

A good rule of thumb is that the more fabric, beading, lace, and embellishment a dress has, the more it's going to cost.

PUTTING IT TOGETHER INTO YOUR BRIDAL STYLE BLUEPRINT

This information will be the foundation of your dress search and a helpful tool to give the consultant at the salon insight into what you are looking for. Fill out the Bridal Style Blueprint worksheet on the following pages or use the **QR code on page 41** to download and create your own Blueprint.

The insight you'll gain through doing this exercise can help as you make decisions on what to buy and how to present yourself to the world in different situations. It is valuable for small purchases and large ones, from big budgets to thrifting, and at every stage in your life. I've noticed it myself as I've watched my style evolve; what felt right to me ten years ago no longer feels like me. On the other hand, I will always love a good Hermès scarf and A-line skirt because that is part of my style DNA. You can come back and redo your Bridal Style Blueprint in the years to come to keep it fresh and relevant to where you are in life.

Second Weddings and Mature Brides

If this isn't your first time walking down the aisle, or if it is and you are at a later stage in life, there is virtually no information out there to help you navigate this process. I love working with clients in these situations because there are so many ways we can help. We often get the following questions from these women, and here are our answers:

- **Can I wear white?** Sometimes older brides (and by that, I mean *my age*!) aren't quite sure what is appropriate to wear. Does wearing white make them seem too youthful? Do they have to if they don't want to? The answer to all of this is *do what feels right to you*. If you've always dreamed of a white dress, then by all means, go for it! Just make sure the style feels appropriate *for you*, whatever your age. For clients in this demographic, I've done everything from chic white gowns to tea-length lace dresses to white tuxedos.
- **Do I have to wear white?** The answer is definitely no! One of my favorite looks that I've done for a bride getting married for a second time was a colorful, embellished evening gown from Oscar de la Renta. It's really about what honors who you are as a woman today.
- **What about a veil?** Whatever feels right to you is what you should do. If you prefer an alternative to a veil, you could explore a fascinator or a hat for a little headpiece drama. Alternatively, we have also done a long sheer cape or a tulle *watteaux* (a piece of fabric coming off the back of the dress) to add sophisticated drama.

THE BRIDAL STYLE BLUEPRINT

Step-By-Step Instructions

In ten minutes you'll have the foundation for dress success! Grab a pen and a nice glass of wine, and let's do this!

1. Answer questions 1–6 by either writing your answers in this book or downloading and filling out the worksheet from the QR code on page 41.
2. Use your answers to complete the Style Summary.
3. Snap a picture of or save your Style Summary and bring it to your dress appointments.

1. The Details

Where and when your wedding is happening plays a large role in the type of dress you select, as does the time of day. It's important to communicate these details so the dress complements your surroundings.

In addition, the formality of your guests' attire is important because you want your dress to coordinate but be more elevated.

The date is:

The ceremony is at (time and venue):

The reception venue is:

The guest dress code is:

- ☐ Black Tie (men in tuxedos and women in long dresses)
- ☐ Formal (men in dark suits and women in long or tea-length dresses)
- ☐ Cocktail (men in suits and women in tea- or knee-length cocktail dresses)
- ☐ Semiformal (men in jackets and ties and women in cocktail dresses)
- ☐ Casual (men in shirts and no tie and women in casual dresses)

2. Personal Style

Contrary to popular belief, personal style is rarely one-dimensional but rather a mix of different elements. I look at it like you have a core style, a supporting style, and a pop of something fun.

Think of it like a cocktail—let's take a vodka soda. You have a main ingredient, vodka (your Core Style); you add in some soda (your Supporting Style); and you finish it off with a twist of lime (your Pop). Personal style is the same thing.

Check the one item that describes you best in each category.

Core Style	Supporting Style	Pop
☐ Bohemian	☐ Bohemian	☐ Sparkle
☐ Casual	☐ Casual	☐ Color
☐ Classic & Elegant	☐ Classic & Elegant	☐ Drama
☐ Edgy & Modern	☐ Edgy & Modern	☐ Sexiness
☐ Feminine & Girly	☐ Feminine & Girly	☐ Glamour
☐ Glamorous & Sexy	☐ Glamorous & Sexy	☐ Trendiness
☐ Minimal	☐ Minimal	☐ Other:
☐ Menswear Inspired	☐ Menswear Inspired	

3. Dress Elements

Embellishments

What kind of details do you gravitate toward? These are often the same as what you like on a wedding dress. For example, do you have a few sequin dresses in your closet? How about lace? While most women don't wear these things on a day-to-day basis, special occasion dressing is a great indicator of the details you like.

Check all of the embellishments that you like.

- ☐ Tonal Shimmer
- ☐ Blingy Sparkle
- ☐ Embroidery
- ☐ Floral Appliques
- ☐ Point d'Esprit
- ☐ Lace
- ☐ Horsehair
- ☐ Color
- ☐ Textured/Printed Fabric
- ☐ Feathers

Fabric

Most wedding dress fabrics fall into one of four categories. Select one or two that appeal to you most.

Check the fabric categories that you like the most (max 2).

- ☐ Structured Silks: faille, mikado, satin
- ☐ Light & Flowery: tulle, organza, chiffon
- ☐ Drippy Silks: charmeuse, satin-backed crêpe
- ☐ Lace or Embroidery

4. Body Type

I know what you're thinking: "I'm gonna tone up, slim down, and look FAB on my wedding day!"

I'm not saying you shouldn't, BUT buying a dress for your future self is *risky*. Who needs that pressure, especially these days? Choose a dress you feel great in today, and it can always be taken in.

Select:

- *One feature you like to accentuate and label it with an* A
- *One feature you like to minimize and label it with an* M

___ Top Half

___ Shoulders

___ Arms

___ Bust

___ Back

___ Bottom Half

___ Waist

___ Legs

___ Thighs

Remember, your partner fell in love with you and asked for your hand the way you are today.

You are beautiful as you are.

5. Dress Shape

Figuring out which silhouette you like the most can be tricky, so look to your closet for clues. What do you typically like to wear? Which shapes are you most drawn to? These are the tried-and-true elements to look for in a wedding dress.

Select the shapes most common in your closet.

Skirts & Dresses	Neckline	Sleeve
☐ Straight	☐ V-Neck	☐ Long
☐ A-Line	☐ Off-the-Shoulder	☐ Cap/Short
☐ Flowy	☐ Crew Neck	☐ Sleeveless

I am also interested in exploring these styles:

☐ Full Skirt/Ball Gown

☐ Strapless Bodice

☐ Overskirt

☐ Cape

☐ Other: ______________________________

Just as important, what do you not want? I wouldn't be caught dead wearing a dress that's

____

____

6. Budget

Today, brides have so many resources to get a dress they love at any budget, but it's important to determine what yours is in advance to be sure you are going to the right stores. There's nothing worse than falling in love with a dress that's too expensive. So, it's important that you clearly communicate your budget from the get-go.

My budget is:

☐ Under $3,000

☐ $3,000 to $5,000

☐ $5,000 to $7,000

☐ $7,000 to $10,000

☐ $10,000+

STYLE SUMMARY

1. Your Details

I am getting married on ______________________ at ______________________,

and the dress code is ______________________.

2. Personal Style

My core style is ______________________,

my supporting style is ______________________,

and a detail I love is a pop of ______________________.

3. Dress Elements

The embellishments that matter to me are ______________________

______________________.

The fabric that appeals to me most is ______________________.

4. Body Type

The part of my body that I tend to like to accentuate is my ______________________,

and I like to minimize my ______________________.

5. Dress Shape

I feel the best when I am wearing a/an ______________________ shape dress

with a ______________________ neckline and a ______________________ sleeve.

I am also open to exploring these styles: ______________________.

6. Budget

The budget I am most comfortable with is between ______________________.

I can go up to $ ______________________ if it's really spectacular.

Congratulations!

You have completed your Bridal Style Blueprint!

You are well on your way to wedding dress success.

I am so excited for you because your Style Summary is going to be a valuable tool in your dress search. Don't forget to bring it with you when you shop.

TRANSLATING ALL THIS INFORMATION INTO YOUR WEDDING STYLE

Now that you have identified your signature style, body shape, and details that you like to wear, it's time to curate a list of designers that design for you. Because I have been doing this for many years, I can quickly identify them for my clients. Just by listening closely during their Style Consultation, I intrinsically know which designers are right for each bride and can often predict the designer they will ultimately purchase from. I am aware that is not something a new bride can do, so I have broken down the process of how to identify the top three designers *for you*.

If I had to guess, you have already begun scrolling Instagram, looking for wedding dresses with varying degrees of success. Maybe this has been fun, but you might have found it to be overwhelming and stressful. Going down the rabbit hole of scrolling without a targeted plan can be frustrating and leave you more confused than when you started.

For example, there is very little connection between looking at something on a 6-foot-tall model and knowing what it will look like on your shape. Same thing with details from a multimillion-dollar wedding that you hope you can recreate on a budget. Instagram provides inspiration but lacks reality.

As much as I would love to go on about how detrimental social media can be to your self-esteem and how it sets up unrealistic expectations, that is all common knowledge. Therefore, I want to teach you how to use it as a tool, albeit one that should be utilized carefully. The good news is that you have already done the heavy lifting of identifying what you like (the hardest part, believe me), and that is the foundation that we will use to curate your vision and home in on the designers you want to explore.

HOW TO USE SOCIAL MEDIA *SMARTLY*

Knowing which platforms to use—and when and how to use them—is going to go a long way when it comes to saving both time and sanity. Below are my tips.

Step 1: Pinterest

About the platform: When it comes to all forms of wedding planning, there is no better platform than Pinterest. A whopping 40 million brides and grooms consult the site to plan their weddings, using over 900 million wedding-related pins at any given time. So what does this have to do with fashion? Thirty-eight million of these pins are images of dresses alone. Don't panic! We are going to show you how to narrow that down significantly.

Why it's great: Contrary to popular belief, Pinterest is not a social media platform like Facebook or Instagram but more of a search engine like Google. This site's USP lies in its ability to return highly relevant search results—a lot of them—quickly. The algorithm moves fast to align with your tastes, curating a gallery of recommended pins you're more likely to enjoy. Organization is a painless task thanks to an almost effortless filing system that saves pins under files you create.

The challenge: While Pinterest has some great images, they are only images, and usually ones that are professionally shot. This means you get very little detail on the dress beyond what you see in a pin. Sometimes they are linked to the source, but that takes you off in a whole different direction.

How to search effectively:

1. **Be specific:** When it comes to searching, details matter—literally. For example, let's say that your Bridal Blueprint revealed that you love long sleeves, lace, and an A-line skirt. Oh, and you love a little pop of sparkle. That's exactly what you need to search for: a long-sleeved lace wedding dress with an A-line skirt and sparkle. It may seem obvious, but a vast majority of brides never get further than a long-sleeved lace dress. You can see how different the results will be!
2. **Go on a Pinning Spree:** This is your time to go crazy and have fun! Pin everything that appeals to you. Don't worry if it's not exactly in your wheelhouse; if there is something about it that you like, Pin It.
3. **Take a break:** Once you have spent a good amount of time pinning (thirty minutes to an hour is good), log off and let it marinate. A few hours or days later, go in and take away things that no longer resonate with you.
4. **Analyze the data:** Having a lot of beautiful images is great, but if you don't know what to do with them, which most brides don't, it doesn't mean anything. The first thing I want you to do is to pay attention to the patterns and what you saved more than once. On almost every board I look at there are multiple saves of the same dress, and sometimes the bride doesn't even realize it. This is a good thing—it means that you're heading in the right direction.
5. **Find your designers:** Now, pull up the worksheet from this section because I want you to write down the name of every dress designer that is on your board.

Each time you have a dress from a designer Pinned, put a mark next to their name. Now tally up who has the most points and use the top three as your focus.

Step 2: Instagram

About the platform: A visual-based social media platform with a powerful link to brands, Instagram is fantastic for investigation and shopping. In fact, it's the most powerful social commerce platform in the world, with over 130 million active shoppers every month. This means brands spend a lot of time, money, and effort on creating content that will showcase designs beyond just a pretty picture.

Why it's great: Instagram is a great research tool for brides who know what designers they are interested in and want to explore what else they have to offer. With Reels, videos, insights, and comments from other consumers, it's a terrific way to find out if the designer you like has a dress you love—and is a brand that shares your values.

The challenge: The biggest setbacks are because the search results are based on the hashtags created by the user, and let's face it: Not everyone (or even most people) knows how to effectively tag a post. That is why Instagram is Step 2 on this list: It's great for a deep dive once you know what you are looking for.

How to search effectively:

1. First things first, grab your list of designers and plug their names into the search bar. Once in their gallery, ask yourself the following questions:
    - Do I identify with this designer?
    - Am I able to get a sense of the personality of the designer from their Stories?
    - What are some of the other styles I like?
2. Next, I want you to look at their tagged posts. These are going to give you a better insight into what the dresses look like on real brides.
3. **Create a folder:** You can do this by choosing an image and hitting the save button. It will ask for a collection name, and you can start saving all of the designs you like in one place.
4. **Use hashtags . . . wisely:** Remember what I said about details? Throw them into your search, and you can often cut through the noise much more quickly. For example, at the time of writing this #longsleevelaceweddingdress has 1,397 posts whereas #longsleeveweddingdress has 68,179, and #laceweddingdress has 436,319 posts.

Step 3: The Designer's Website

It's funny, but in the era of social media, brides don't always think to use the designer's website as part of their search. This is often because people find it easier to scroll through Instagram than to click on photos on their computer. However, the website can be really useful because you will get much more in-depth information and photos, see their full collection, and often find options that you didn't see on social media. You can also find out which stores their dresses are sold in (called Stockists) and when their trunk shows are.

In the next chapter, we are going to do a deep dive into the specifics you'll want to be familiar with before shopping, such as fabric, dress shape, and sleeve options.

Scan this QR code for additional resources from this chapter.

Chapter 3

WEAVES, SLEEVES, AND SILHOUETTES

AS WITH ALMOST EVERYTHING in the world of weddings (and life), finding the perfect dress and building a great wedding wardrobe begins with smart research and planning. I highly recommend shopping for your dress as you would do any other meaningful task—with dedication, seriousness, and passion! To do that, you'll need a basic understanding of wedding dress fabrics, silhouettes, sleeves, and waistlines.

This section is intended to be used as a reference guide, and having these terms at the ready will come in handy throughout your shopping journey. Most importantly, they will help you make informed decisions while saving you time, energy, and sanity. Let's start the crash course!

A GUIDE TO FABRICS

When thinking about wedding dress fabrics, it's not uncommon for brides to focus on the initial look and feel. But it's important to also consider things like durability, weight, thickness, and appropriateness for both the weather and the venue. I once spoke to a bride that was so hot on her wedding day that the sweat was dripping down her arms and legs during the ceremony, creating stains on her gorgeous duchesse satin dress. Needless to say, she changed into her reception dress as fast as she could!

The bottom line: Choose fabrics that can handle the demands of the location and activity planned for your big day. I will focus here on the most commonly found wedding dress fabrics.

Charmeuse: Known for its beautiful drape and illustrious shine, charmeuse is made from silk or polyester and is a lightweight fabric with a satin weave and matte backing.

Chiffon: A lightweight gauzy fabric, chiffon flows beautifully and has a sheer appearance. It can be made of silk, polyester, cotton, nylon, or rayon. It also comes in a crinkle version that provides texture.

Crêpe: Crêpe has a distinct thickness and is made from silk, wool, polyester, or rayon. It drapes beautifully and has a bit of a bumpy texture.

Crêpe back satin (also known as Satin-backed crêpe): This is a lightweight, reversible fabric with a shiny luster on one side and a matte finish on the other. It's celebrated for its versatility as well as its ability to move with the body without getting wrinkled.

Damask: Damask is a jacquard-patterned fabric with a design woven into the fabric as opposed to being printed on it. Damask can be made from silk, linen, cotton, wool, polyester, or rayon.

Double-faced satin: Created on specially designed looms, double-faced satin has a thick, luxurious hand-feel. It is a fabric with two "right sides," meaning it looks the same from every angle and doesn't require a lining. This allows designers to be more creative in how they use it without adding weight to the dress.

Duchesse satin: Known for its shiny luster and high thread count, duchesse satin drapes beautifully because of its stiffness. It's been a longtime favorite of the Royal Family (hence the name) and haute couture houses for evening wear and bridal gowns.

Faille: A woven fabric with a slightly ribbed texture, faille is traditionally made with silk and has a matte appearance. It is a durable light- to medium-weight fabric that can hold its shape and can be worn in any season, making it a favorite of bridal designers.

Gazar: Similar to organza (but with a heavier weight and less sheer), gazar silk is a stiff fabric that holds its shape and is often used for ball gowns, dresses with full skirts, and more structured designs.

Georgette: Georgette is a beautiful flowy fabric with a matte appearance that can be made from a variety of fibers. When made from silk, it resembles less sheer chiffon. There are several iterations of georgette, including double georgette, which is thicker than the others; satin georgette, which has a shiny luster; and stretch georgette.

Jersey: A smooth, stretchy fabric popularized by Coco Chanel, silk jersey fabric is breathable and comfortable with a strong drape effect. It is often used for more figure-hugging designs.

Lace: Lace is a delicate and romantic fabric usually used as an overlay or detail in wedding dresses. In the past, it was made from silk and linen, but in modern times it can be made from cotton, polyester, and rayon by hand or machine.

Mikado: Also called Zibeline, it is a crisp, pure woven fabric made of silk or wool-silk blend. Because it is a structured fabric with high durability and an elegant sheen, it's commonly used in wedding dresses.

Organza: Lightweight, shimmery, and sheer, organza is a plain-woven fabric with a structured drape that works well for full-skirted dresses. There is also a satin-faced version that is more opaque and has a gorgeous luster. It's one of my favorites!

Pique: The distinctive characteristic of a pique fabric is the tiny geometric pattern in the weave. It takes an ordinary fabric like cotton, or, in the case of wedding dresses, silk, and gives the fabric a stiffness and textured feel without adding weight. In fact, pique is often considered to be good in warm temperatures because the open weave allows air to flow through it and keep the wearer cool.

Point d'esprit: A type of dotted tulle. Its polka-dot design makes it a bit heavier with less drape than other tulles. The simple-weave dots can be made tiny and dainty or larger. This fabric is also called Swiss Dot.

Taffeta: While getting a bad rap as being an eighties cliché ("friends don't let friends wear taffeta"), it can actually be a beautiful and highly functional fabric because it is crisp, lightweight, and drapes beautifully. Today, it is also available in less expensive poly versions.

Tulle: A delicate, sheer fabric, tulle is often used to make veils and flowy, ethereal wedding dresses. It can be made from silk, nylon, or polyester, with silk being the rarest and most fragile, making it the most luxurious choice.

Organza

Mikado

Lace

Jersey

Gazar

Charmeuse

Chiffon

Pique

Point d'Esprit

Taffeta

Tulle

Faille

Duchesse Satin

Double-Faced Satin

Damask

Crêpe Back Satin

Crêpe

French Lace

Northern France is known to house the best leavers lacemaking machines in the world. And, like champagne, only lace made a certain way—in France—can be called French lace. Leavers lace is the most intricate and luxurious lace in the world.

There are four types of lace that are frequently used in wedding dresses:

1. **Alençon:** Using Chantilly lace as its base, Alençon lace has cording added onto the pattern to create a 3D effect. It originated in the town of Alençon in Northern France in the sixteenth century and continues to be one of the most widely used laces today. It is a popular choice for wedding dresses as it comes in many patterns and sizes.
2. **Chantilly:** The most delicate of all French lace, it is a non-corded lace that is thin and soft and is frequently used with other laces to add dimension and texture.
3. **Lyon:** The most luxurious in the group, it is usually larger and has more detail in the pattern. The crème de la crème of French lace, its characteristics include larger scale, pattern complexity, and multiple gradients (i.e., size and types of holes weaved in the pattern).
4. **Guipure:** Heavy and dense with a distinct pattern, this lace does not have a mesh background and is instead held together by bars or plaits that connect the motifs.

Why Do Brides Wear White?

Brides have always worn wedding colors associated with their culture and customs. Ancient Roman brides wore *flammea* (veils) in deep yellow to represent the color of a flame—likely why actress Elizabeth Taylor chose to wear yellow at her first wedding to Sir Richard Burton, whom she fell in love with in Rome. Ancient Greek women wore red.

Though other royal women wore white for their weddings before her, it wasn't until the 1840 marriage of Queen Victoria to her first cousin Prince Albert that the modern version of the "white wedding dress" became the standard for Western brides.

Until Victoria's wedding, Western brides of the middle and lower classes simply wore their "best dress" when they got married. This was usually one they could re-wear and made in a color that would be suitable for other important occasions. At times, women would choose gray, black, and light purple (suitable for mourning), but the most common colors were russet and brown. Those of a more aristocratic background often wore jewel tones with gold embroidery and sometimes fur and lace, and royal brides leaned toward silver, gold, and red to showcase their regal background.

So, why did Queen Victoria opt for white? There are a few theories. One is that she felt the color showed off the beautiful Honiton lace that adorned her Spitalfields cream silk-satin dress. Another is that the impracticality of white signified her wealth and status in a way that was less obvious than the bolder (more practical) tones. What we *do* know for sure is that it had nothing to do with virginity or innocence. In fact, blue was the color most associated with purity and faithfulness because of its link to the Virgin Mary.

So, for any of you with family members or future in-laws with something to say about you wearing white to your second wedding, while pregnant, or after you have had a baby, send them a history book and continue with your plan to wear what you want!

DRESS SHAPE

LEARNING YOUR SILHOUETTES

While you might have a silhouette in mind for your wedding dress, I highly encourage you to choose a few different ones to try on as well. I cannot tell you how often brides try on the dress shape they think will look great on them, only to find that it just doesn't look right on their body, and then end up with the exact thing they said they didn't want.

A-Line: An A-line dress is fitted at the waist and transitions into a gentle *A* shape as it moves down the body. Universally favored as the most flattering of all the silhouettes, this classic shape is a timeless choice which is why, unsurprisingly, it's the most popular style of dress year after year. An A-line creates a slim waistline, and lengthens the body, making it a wonderful option for brides who wish to highlight these areas and hide wider hips and softer bellies.

Ball Gown: The ultimate "fairy tale" silhouette, the ball gown has a large, voluminous skirt and is the quintessential wedding dress shape. Because of its grandeur, it works well in a large house of worship or dramatic setting. Brides choose ball gowns for various reasons, but they are particularly flattering if you want to minimize your bottom half and accentuate your waist.

Column: A column skirt hangs straight from the waist without a flare at the bottom or a train. They are often used in bridal gowns when there is an overskirt attached to them.

Mermaid: A mermaid shape is a slim silhouette that nips in at the knee and flares out below. It's perfect for brides who want to show off their curves (or create the illusion of having some) because this shape really highlights the body. One word of caution: It can be a bit restrictive, so be sure to move around, sit down, and do a few dance moves during your fittings!

Princess: A princess cut is when a dress does not have a seam at the waist but instead has two seams going down the front of the gown. This creates a long and lean line and is very flattering on many shapes. Some princess gowns have volume in the skirt, while others don't have any at all.

Sheath: A beautiful and more practical alternative to the slip dress, a sheath silhouette hugs the body, often nipping in at the waist without having a defined waist seam. It's classically beautiful and particularly appealing to those who want to appear taller and leaner.

Trumpet: Brides often confuse mermaid and trumpet shapes because they are both slim through the hip, but a trumpet shape flares out higher (typically mid-thigh) while a mermaid flares out at or below the knee. A trumpet shape can look good on many body types and is a fantastic option for brides who don't want to have a large skirt but also don't want something restrictive.

What Is a Train?

A train is the fabric in the back of a dress or skirt that extends past where the hem hits the floor and trails behind the garment. Up until approximately the Roaring Twenties, trains were commonplace in women's attire. Today, it's very possible that your wedding dress is the only time you will ever wear a train, as they are only reserved for the most formal occasions and wedding dresses. So here is a quick guide to the different train lengths you will find when dress shopping.

Cathedral: They are 22 inches past where the back of the dress hits the floor and pretty much the longest of the train lengths we see in wedding dresses today (except, of course, Princess Diana's famous 25-foot train!).

Chapel: Measuring between 12 inches and 18 inches past where the back of the dress hits the floor, these trains are the most common version used today. They are more manageable than a long cathedral train, but still have the dramatic "bridal" feel that most women want.

Sweep: A sweep train has just a few inches of fabric past where the back of the dress hits the floor. These are most common on evening gowns and should be carefully considered before wearing. If left on the floor while dancing or walking in a crowded room, they very easily get stepped on and ripped—and even cause the wearer to trip. However, typically there isn't enough fabric to bustle them up; so my advice to our clients is usually to remove these trains and make the dress floor-length all the way around to avoid an accident.

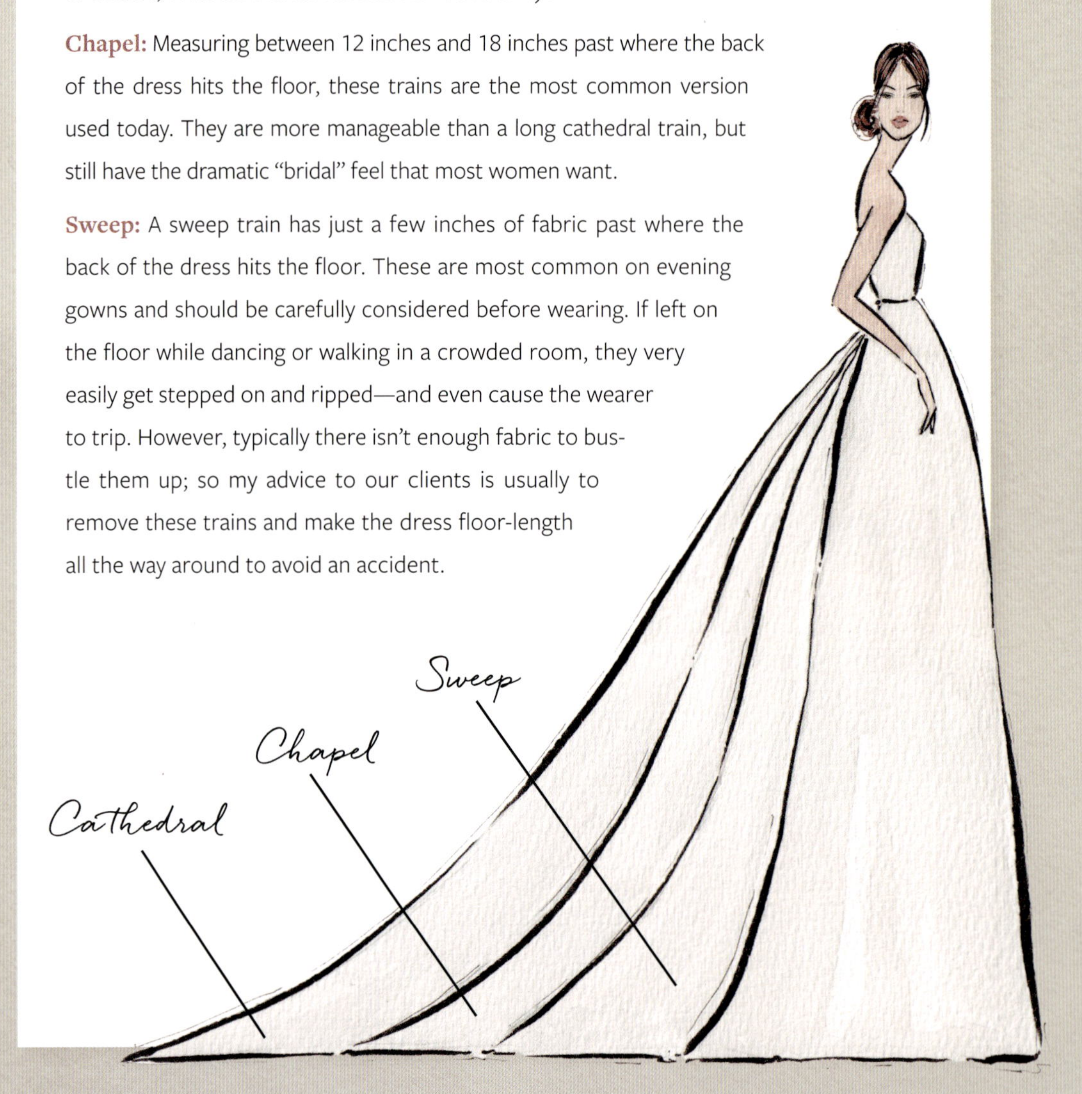

NECKLINES

The neckline of a dress serves as the frame for your face and can have a big impact on your overall look, as necklines have the ability to accentuate curves, elongate the torso, and make shoulders look either wider or narrower. Below are the most common necklines found in bridal wear.

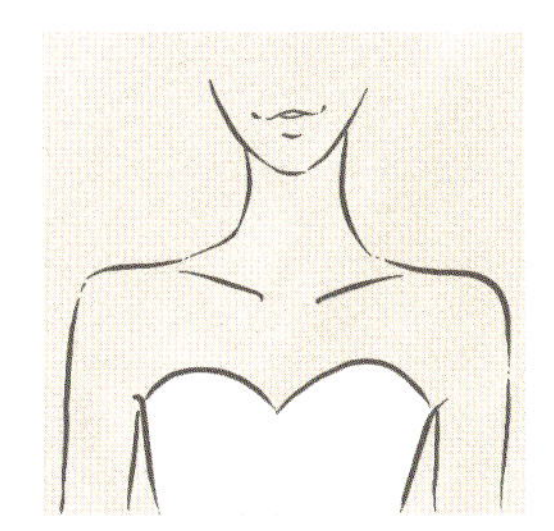

Sweetheart: Named for the way this neckline resembles the top of a heart shape with its rounded half-circles and dipped V between the breasts. I have found over the years that women either love or hate this neckline. It tends to elongate the neck, balance the hips, and flatter many different bust sizes depending on the cut. The depth of the V is an important piece of the equation and, upon request, can often be closed up in production so that it's not as deep. Lowering it can easily be done in fittings.

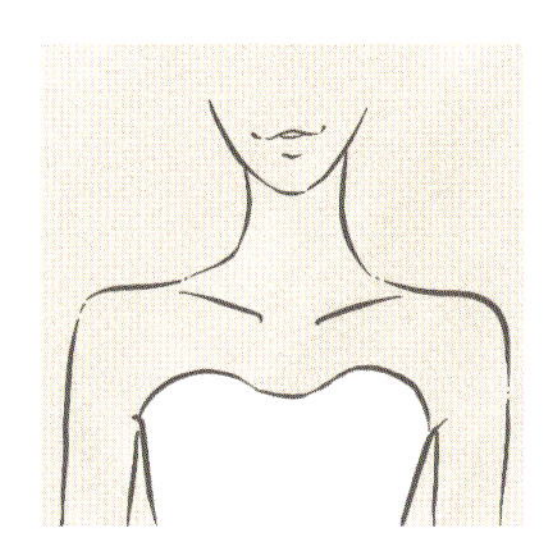

Modified Sweetheart: This is when there is a dip in the bodice but is not a full sweetheart. It's a nice alternative for someone who wants a softer neckline. It's a middle ground between a defined sweetheart and straight-across and can often be created in fittings from a straight neckline.

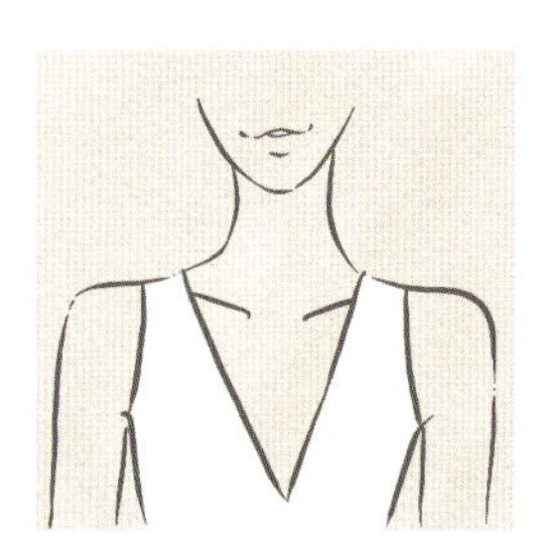

Plunging V: While a bit risqué for some, this neckline is a fantastic choice for brides who want to give the illusion of an elongated torso and who have B- and C-cup breasts. These dresses usually come with illusion tulle paneling, so you get more coverage and security than you might expect.

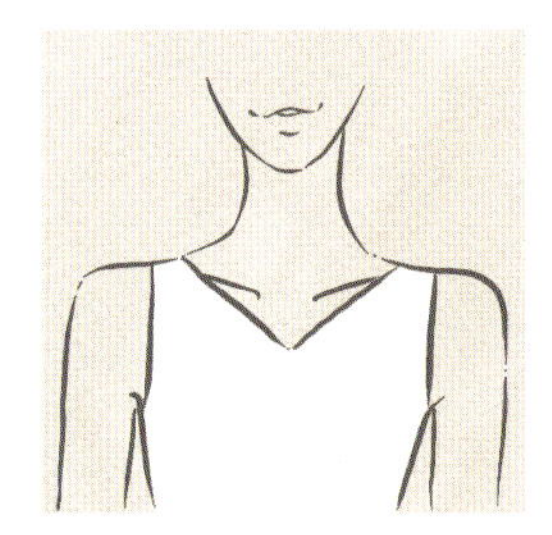

V-Neck: Versatile, a deep V-neck can look sexy, daring, and dramatic, whereas a more demure cut can look almost princess-like. This is an excellent choice for brides who don't want strapless or who want to show off a little cleavage or lengthen their torso.

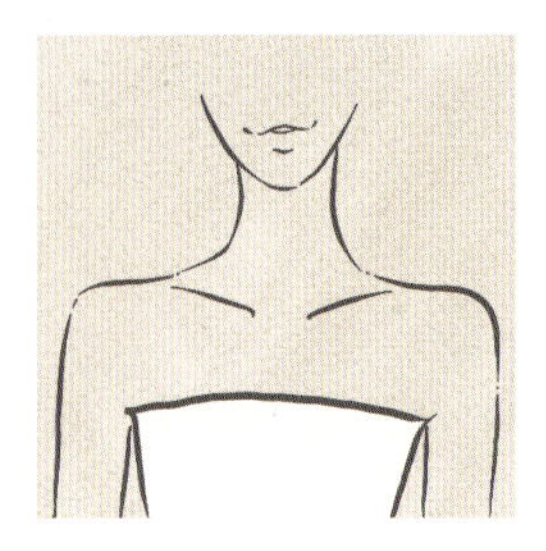

Strapless—Straight-Across: Timeless and sophisticated, the straight neckline highlights the clavicle bone and neck and brings broad shoulders into balance beautifully.

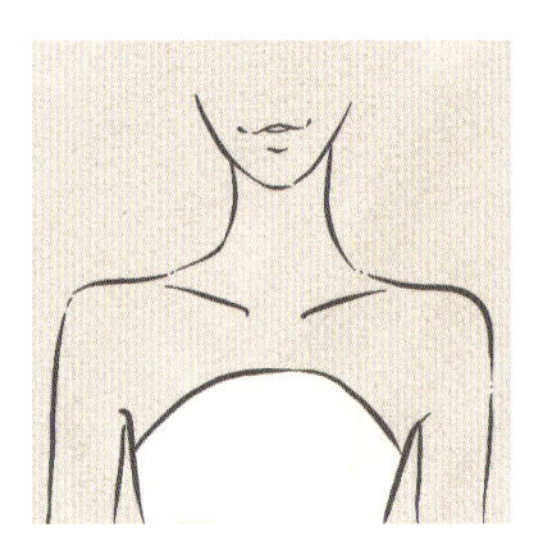

Strapless—Rounded: This neckline is when the bodice goes above the bust in a semicircular curve. It's not very common, but it's incredibly classic and tends to be good on someone with a smaller bust. It's near and dear to my heart since my wedding dress had one!

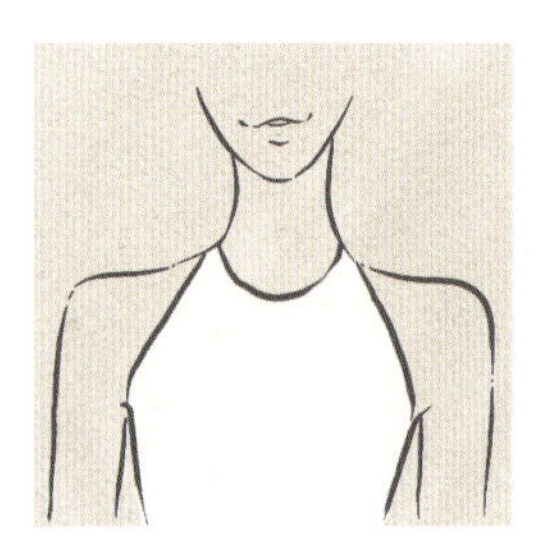

Halter: The shape of the neckline draws the eyes in and up and highlights the shoulders. It's also a great way to enhance curves, especially up top.

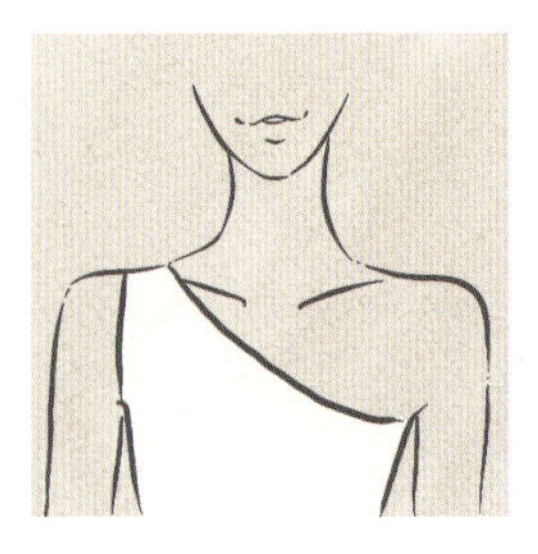

Asymmetrical: Dramatic, glamorous, and suitable for all body types, the one-shoulder neckline draws attention to the top half of the body and is best when accompanied by a great pair of earrings.

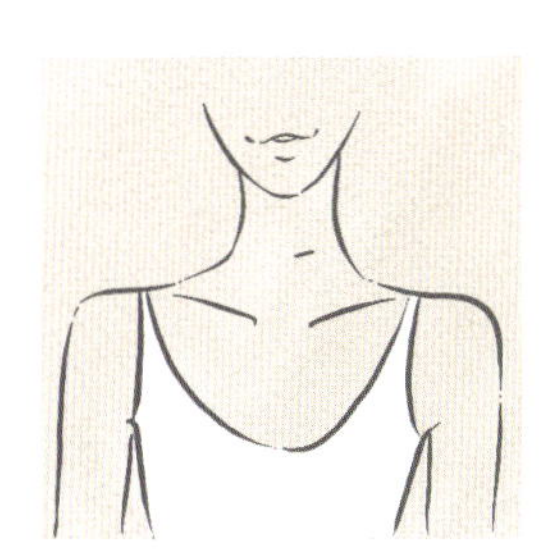

Scoop: The deep scoop in this neckline highlights the face and is flattering on women with either larger or smaller breasts. Sophia Loren vibes on the former, prima ballerina on the latter. It can read a little more on the casual side, but as seen on our beautiful bride above, there is an exception to every rule, as her dress is the epitome of black-tie elegance.

Portrait: Very popular at the moment, a portrait neckline shows the chest and shoulder while wrapping around the arm (and possibly having a sleeve). It's a timeless style that highlights your face and collarbone, and if the sleeve extends low enough, it has the added advantage of hiding the upper arms. I tend to like them most without a large skirt so it's balanced out and does not overwhelm the wearer.

SLEEVES

There are many iterations of sleeves that can be done, and several self-explanatory styles I don't include here, like cap sleeve, three-quarter length, and long sleeve.

Bishop: This sleeve style has been having a *major* comeback recently. Immensely popular from the 1830s to 1860s, these sleeves are narrow at the top, fuller at the bottom, and gathered at the cuff. Today you see them done mostly in sheer fabrics such as tulle or chiffon, but they can also be done in the same fabric as the dress.

Juliet: Hands down the most romantic of the options, the Juliet has a pouf at the shoulder and tapers to a slim sleeve. It can be done in several sleeve lengths and fabrics. We don't see them a lot now, but if you look at dresses from the eighties, they dominate!

Tulip: Named for its resemblance to the flower, this romantic short sleeve overlaps on the arm and gives a dress a romantic and whimsical look.

Illusion: This is usually lace or a stretch tulle that is sheer and is not backed with fabric, so the skin shows through.

Flutter: Sweet and youthful, flutter sleeves aren't much of a sleeve at all because they are short and made by gathering fabric at the seam to create a ruffle or "flutter" around the arm like a butterfly.

SLEEVES

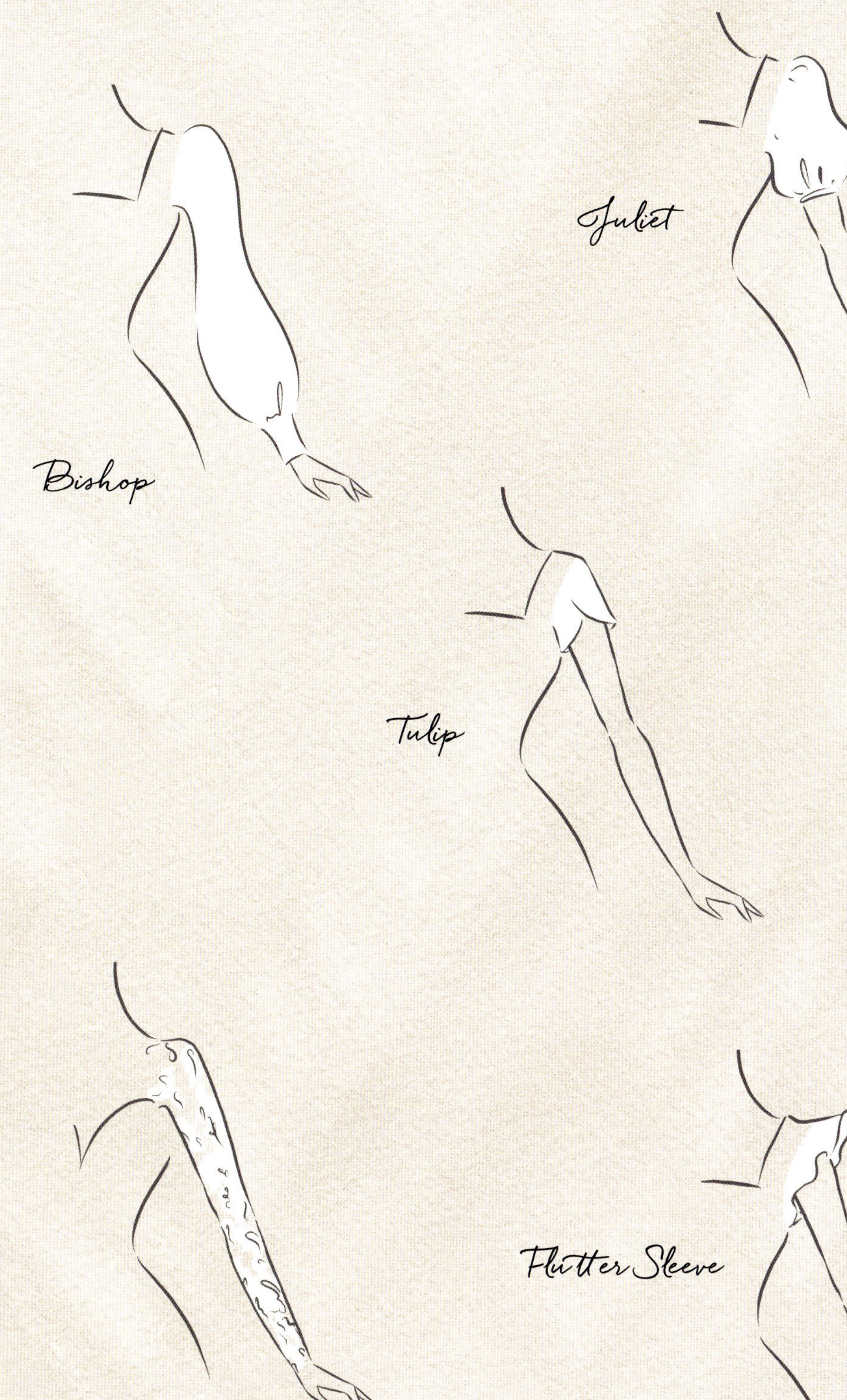

WAISTLINES

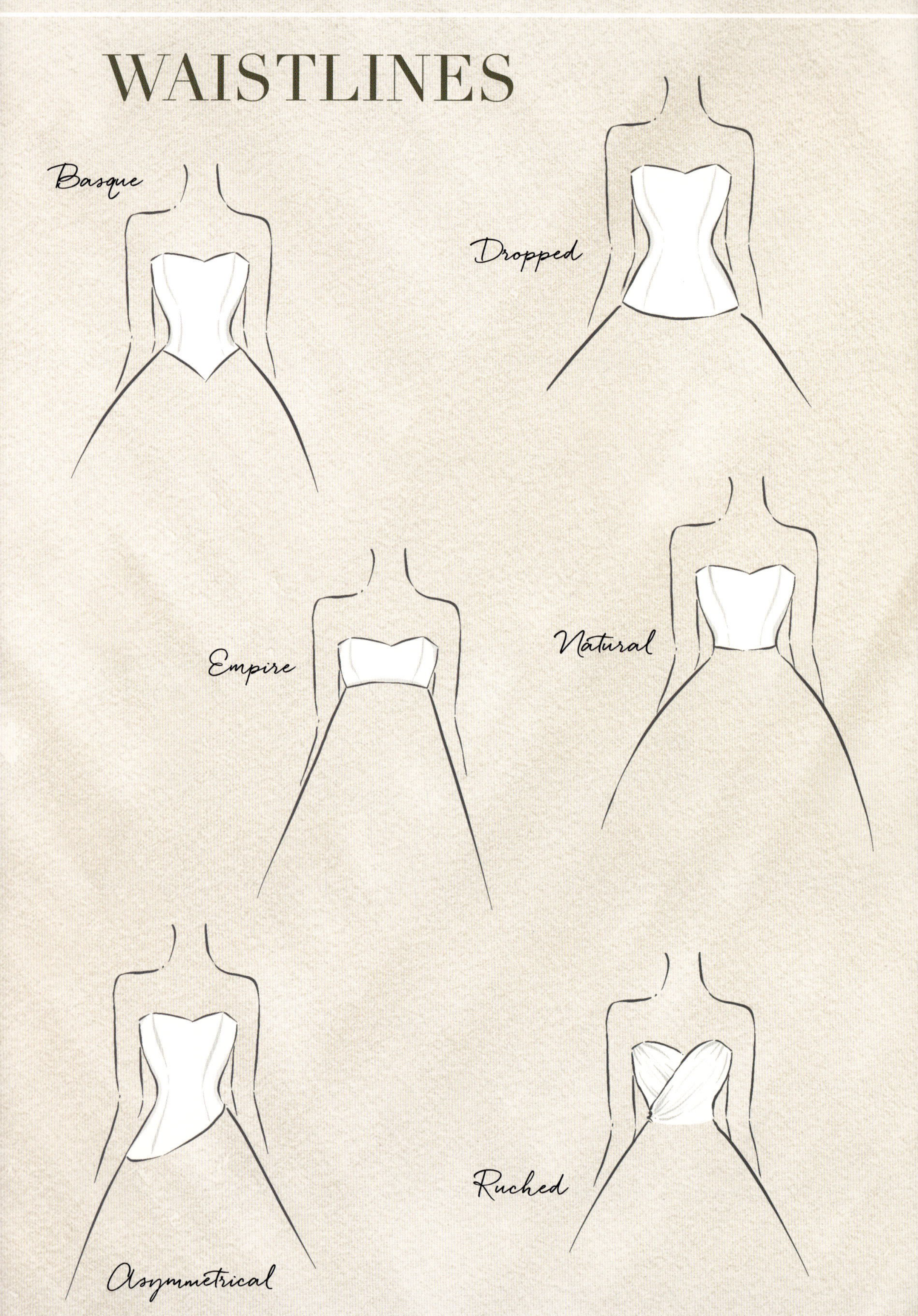

WAISTLINES

Basque: Elongating, feminine, and timeless, this V-waistline is perfect for the bride who wants to look like a princess with an hourglass shape.

Dropped: Incredibly popular in both the 1920s and 1980s, dropped waists are torso-lengtheners but can also make the legs look shorter if they are too severe.

Empire: This shape isn't at the waist at all; it sits right below the bust and often hides a soft (or pregnant) midsection and gives the illusion of height.

Natural: The natural waist falls at the smallest part of a woman's midsection, or "natural waist," and therefore directs the eye right to the narrowest part of the body.

Asymmetrical: Most often found on A-line and trumpet gowns, this waistline draws a line from the waist to the hips and looks great on curves. If you have some to flaunt—or want to create the illusion of some—this is a fantastic option!

Ruched: A ruched waist is made from gathered fabric that is draped across the dress—often asymmetrically—creating a very flattering shape on many body types. And it is my go-to suggestion for women who tend to hold their weight in their midsection.

Now that we have defined your style and defined some of the basics, let's talk about the hardest part: wedding dress sizing.

Scan this QR code for additional resources from this chapter.

Chapter 4

THE TRUTH ABOUT BRIDAL SIZING

IF YOU ARE ANYTHING like I was as I headed to shop for my dress, you envision yourself gleefully making your way to a fabulous boutique where you'll be greeted by a cheerful consultant who's ready to give you their undivided attention. You and your dearest friends will sip champagne, you'll select a few dresses to try (*all* of which will be in your size and budget), and, after trying several on, you'll experience a moment when you know with full certainty that you have found *the one*.

Your mother will cry, your best friend will cheer, and you'll head to lunch to toast your purchase and discuss how gorgeous you will look on your big day. It's a beautiful image and one that I have watched play out in the minds of thousands of brides-to-be. But here's the secret no one shares: It has turned out this way for exactly *none* of them.

While Hollywood writers would have you believe that wedding dress shopping is an awesome, champagne-filled experience, the reality is often much less glamorous—*and often much more stressful*—for most brides. Sure, dress shopping *can* be fun and exciting, but it can also be overwhelming, emotional, and even distressing. This is especially true when brides aren't equipped with the knowledge and tools required to navigate it. This is why it's so important to do your research, set realistic expectations, and choose carefully who you include.

In the next few chapters, I am going to set you up for success by sharing the real deal about what I have learned over the last two decades of wedding dress shopping with my clients. It is my goal to empower you with everything you need to know to help you make the most of your shopping journey.

The first thing I'm going to talk about is what I've found to be the biggest setback for brides when it comes to finding their dress: bridal sizing.

A GUIDE TO BRIDAL SIZING

Sizing can exacerbate body insecurities and wreak havoc on the shopping experience. If my time in this industry has taught me one thing, it is to address these concerns up-front. While wedding dress sizing is a pain point for almost every woman I've ever worked with, it's particularly difficult for women who are on the curvy side (like me) and who already feel left out of the fashion industry. Unfortunately, in many ways these women are set up to fail and feel bad in the process. But don't worry. I am going to teach you how to work within the system and find a dress you love regardless of your shape or size. So, let's get the tough part out of the way first so you can be prepared for what's to come.

Though common sense would suggest otherwise, bridal wear doesn't run true-to-size. In fact, it runs very small—*as in two sizes smaller than regular clothing*! Yes, you read that correctly. If you are a US size 10, you will most likely be a US 14 in bridal, *if not bigger*. If you think that sounds crazy, you're right. As much as I wish it wasn't the case, the number on the tag matters to us as women and affects how we feel about ourselves. I can say with complete certainty that I've never worked with a bride that was happy to order a dress in a much bigger size than what she normally wears.

For me, understanding *why* something happens helps me rationalize it, so in this section, we are going to tease apart this archaic system so that you know what to expect and are armed with tactical ways to deal with it. So let's begin by talking about the history that led us here.

It's all Christian Dior's fault (kind of, not really, but kind of . . .).

Although *haute couture* has been referenced for hundreds of years, it wasn't until Parisian designer Christian Dior showed his first haute couture collection in 1947 that our modern concept of *couture* clothing was born.

Dior's designs were opulent and beautiful, but his cuts were less about comfort and movement and more about creating a sculpted silhouette based on his specific (and exaggerated) ideas of feminine perfection.

This ideal included an impossibly small waist and a narrow torso that turned away from the comfortable, loose-fitting designs introduced by designer Coco Chanel in the 1920s. Unlike Chanel's designs, which relaxed the waistline and allowed women the same movement men enjoyed in their clothing, Dior's dresses required body alterations for even the most petite customer. In fact, he's been credited with singlehandedly ushering in a post-war reintroduction of body modifiers like corsets and girdles.

Coco Chanel was unimpressed. She labeled the designer a chauvinist and was open and liberal with her disapproval. "Dior doesn't dress women. *He upholsters them*," she famously remarked. So horrified by the restrictive designs Dior showcased in his 1954 show, Chanel came out of retirement to give women more form-forgiving options.

What does this have to do with your wedding dress? Well, the cuts and measurements favored by Dior—the ones that were considered old-fashioned and restrictive to the average 1950s woman with her 27.5-inch waist and 34B bra size—*are still being used* for today's woman, who has an average waist size of 34 inches and a bust that fits a 36DD bra.

While I believe it's not the designer's intention to do so, this antiquated sizing system based on European size charts can wreak havoc on a woman's psyche. Many larger ready-to-wear clothing brands have adjusted with the times, but generally those in the designer fashion and wedding dress industries have stuck with the old sizing methods. Why? you ask. The truth is hard to get to, but one argument is that wedding dresses are altered anyway, so the sizing number doesn't matter. Another is that every designer has a different size chart that coordinates with its patterns, and they are difficult to change. No matter what the reason, it can be incredibly difficult for a woman at this vulnerable moment in her life when she wants to look her absolute best.

The pressure on today's woman is exacerbated by images of perfection on social media and a society that continues to not only value thinness but also *devalue* curves. As a result, many women find having to order a dress that's two to three sizes larger embarrassing. It can be particularly distressing if you're one of the 67 percent, or 200 million American women, who are considered "plus size" but may not embrace that label.[1]

How Measurements Translate to Size

To complicate matters even more, there isn't an industry standard of sizing, and each company has its own size chart that's specific to its dresses; you could easily be a 12 with one designer and a 16 with another. I'm sure that you've experienced the frustration when trying on regular clothing that one brand's size 8 is another's 4. And even more frustrating, within the same designer, one style often fits differently from another. It's maddening!

With wedding dresses, the semantics of the terminology make it even more confusing. You are told by the designer or store that the dress is "made for you" and your measurements are taken, so many brides naturally assume that the dress will be made for her and to her specifications. But what it actually means is that, in order to determine your size in their dresses, the store will take measurements (typically bust, waist, and hip) and put you in the size that works the best for you. Of course, there isn't an industry standard of sizing, and each company has its own size chart that's specific to its dresses. The reason that your size may be so much bigger than what you typically wear is that the dress has to be ordered according to your biggest measurement of the three: bust, waist, or hip. You might be a size 10 on top and a 14 on the bottom,

1 Gitnux, "The Most Surprising Plus Size Industry Statistics and Trends in 2023," *Market Data* (blog), last edited March 23, 2023, https://blog.gitnux.com/plus-size-industry-statistics. See also "Closing the Representation Gap for Plus-Size Women," *The Takeaway* (blog), podcast with Amanda M. Czerniawski, WNYC Studios, September 27, 2016, https://www.wnycstudios.org/podcasts/takeaway/segments/closing-representation-gap-plus-size-women.

Lessons from a Real Bride

Victoria stood in the dressing room, her curvy 5-foot-2, 165-pound body stuck in a size 4 wedding dress sample she couldn't move in, let alone get off. Embarrassed and scared, she started to sweat, fearing she would stain the dress, or worse, have to be cut out of it in front of everyone in the salon. She could hear the consultant speaking to her manager a few feet away as her best friend tried to console her through the curtain.

"It was the most humiliating experience of my life," she says. Though the consultant was able to get her out of the dress, the damage was done. "I pushed my wedding date because I was traumatized by the experience. I couldn't go back into a salon for a long time and it's something I share so that other brides don't have the same experience," she says.

but they have to order you a size 14 so that it fits everywhere. Then, when the dress arrives, the larger-size top will be altered to fit you during the fitting process.

Occasionally, designers can do what is called a "split size," in which they order the top in one size and the bottom in another. If you find there is a large difference between your top and bottom sizes, definitely ask if they can do a split-size order for you.

All of this is to show that these numbers are fairly arbitrary. Therefore, when it comes to ordering your wedding dress, prepare yourself in advance to not care about the number. Put it out of your mind and don't give the number any power to affect your self-esteem.

Lastly, you should also know up-front that if your measurements fall over a size 14 on their size chart, you are almost always asked to pay an upcharge of somewhere between 10 to 25 percent depending on how large the dress size is. Brands say the reason for these policies from designers is that they need to make the pattern larger to accommodate the size and that the dress requires more materials to make. While there is a certain reality to that, it can also feel like you are being punished or paying a penalty for your weight. I've had clients find this so discriminatory and exclusionary that they have refused to purchase a dress from designers with this policy. I understand both sides of the coin, but I very much wish for a solution that doesn't feel so terrible to a curvy woman.

DRESS SAMPLE SIZES

While the bridal sizing system is less than ideal, the real issue brides face isn't the number on the tag of the dress; it's that in the world of designer wedding dresses, *the vast majority* of women will not fit into the sample dresses at the store.

The deal is this: Wedding dress samples are expensive for the store to purchase, and therefore, most stores only have one sample of each dress. In an effort to make that sample work on as many women as possible, the majority of them are ordered in a bridal size 8 or 10 (a ready-to-wear 4 or 6) with a B cup. Conceptually this makes sense because it is in the middle of the designers' size charts, which only go up to a size 14, but the data shows that 68 percent of American women wear a size 14 or above.[2] For these women, trying on a bridal size 8 isn't going to work. Even if they can get the dress on their body, they won't really be able to tell what it is going to look like when it fits. But this can also be hard for a very thin or petite woman because, when the sample is way too big, all the clamping in the world won't help them know how it will look in their size. The bottom line is that unless you are 5-foot-8 and a size 4/6 with a B cup, you are going to run into some challenges.

2 Hilary George-Parkin, "Size, by the Numbers," Racked, June 5, 2018, https://www.racked.com/2018/6/5/17380662/size-numbers-average-woman-plus-market.

Get ready to try on a lot of dresses that don't fit.

You now know that you will most likely not be trying on a sample dress that fits perfectly. This means if you are short, busty, have wide hips, a short torso, or wear a larger size, you're going to be trying on a lot of dresses that don't fit. If you know this going in, you can be prepared to use a good amount of imagination to envision what the dress is going to look like. Here are a few tips that I hope will help.

Quick Tip: Be Mindful of Trunk Show Promises!

Trunk show dresses are even smaller because they're made for very tall, very thin models to wear on the runway. I once had a size 2 bride cry when she couldn't get her arms into a trunk show sample. It was an awful moment, and I told the designer about it.

Petite

If you are petite, it's no surprise that many of the sample dresses in the shop are going to be *very long*. While most stores will provide pedestals for you to stand on, this also causes a bit of an issue in that it makes your legs look longer so you don't get an accurate idea of how the dress actually suits your body. To circumvent this, I recommend that you fold the hem underneath so you can get an idea of the dress in your correct length and how each area falls on *your* body.

The other issue with extra length is that the excess fabric makes the skirt appear to have more volume at the bottom than it will when the dress is altered to fit you. It can be hard to fold all the layers of a ball gown underneath, but do give it a try and take a picture so you can be sure that you like it on you.

Finally, if the dress is made on a 5-foot-10 form and you are 5-foot-2, it may be too long at the waist, or the break in the skirt (where the fabric flares out) may hit lower than it should. Have a conversation with your consultant about these and any other concerns, and make sure that they can be adjusted, either in production or fittings.

Busty

If you have a larger bust, there is a good chance the wedding dress sample won't fully zip up, making it harder to visualize the final look. Most designers can give more room by "opening the cup" in production, but this means you're going to have to use your imagination. You will also need to consider how much support the dress offers, as a B cup needs less support than a D cup, and as every bride is different in terms of breast size, shape, and what she finds comfortable, you may not have what you need. There are lots of ways to add bust support that we will talk about later—wearing a longline corset, taping them in place, and adding cups to the dress—but you will want to discuss your options for each particular dress with the consultant (and maybe a Dress Fitter if the consultant doesn't seem well versed in the topic), so you know what to expect.

Petite and Busty

If you are someone who happens to be both petite and busty, you are facing both challenges above, and it's not easy. For some reason the assumption the fashion industry makes is that as your size gets bigger you also get taller, which is just not the case. Why is it that the waist of a size 12 dress is likely at least a good 1" lower than the size 2? This isn't necessarily a deal-breaker when trying on a dress because you can usually just pull up the waist seam so it's in the right spot, but it is something to keep in mind when analyzing if you like the overall shape of the dress itself.

Thin

If you are a woman who has a very small frame and is very thin, the challenge in trying on dresses is that they are all going to be massive on you. That means that the seams won't be sitting in the right place, and even with our tricks of the trade, it may be hard to see what it will look like on your frame. For you, my recommendation is to track down trunk shows because those samples are straight from the runway and fit to a model. They will still be long, but at least they will be proportionally better for you.

Curvy

The challenge curvy women face is that, depending on the shape of the dress and the size they wear, they may not be able to try the sample on at all. I've been to many appointments over the years where the dress is held up to the women so they can attempt to get an idea of what it will look like. This is so hard, and most women don't feel comfortable purchasing a dress that they can't try on.

If you are considering an A-line or ball gown shape, you may be able to put the dress on and just not have it zip up in the back. While this is far from ideal, you will be able to get an idea of what it looks like on your body.

A Few Helpful Tools

There are a few tailoring/dressmaking items that can help a consultant "size" a dress to show the bride what it will look like when it fits in their size. These methods aren't perfect and by no means replace a great-fitting sample, but they do help.

However, many stores don't have these tools or if they do, they are ugly and in distracting colors. So I created the **Sample Size Solution** to be a resource for all parties involved. The

product kit is popular with brides of all sizes and used by consultants at boutiques all over the country. It includes:

Clips and clamps: When a dress doesn't fit, the consultant can use clamps (which come in two sizes) to cinch in the waist, shorten the straps, or add extra support to a dress.

A panel of fabric: One of the worst experiences for a bride is when a dress doesn't zip and they have to model it for their family and friends with the back wide open. It happened to me, and it was humiliating. A simple panel of ivory fabric provides coverage in the back and can be secured with the aforementioned clamps.

Elastic bands: On their own, elastic bands don't do much, but when used with two clamps, they can hold the dress together in the back. This means the consultant doesn't have to hold everything closed and try to duck out of the picture. If you add in the panel of fabric, you really have something that's a useful and effective tool to help brides envision what a dress will really look like.

You can purchase the product kit on our website.

Final Tip: If you fall into any of the categories we spoke about in the preceding section, it will be helpful to tell the store in advance. They may have a consultant that is knowledgeable about working with your particular shape and size and, most importantly, will be sensitive to how you feel.

USE YOUR IMAGINATION

There's nothing that matches the experience of slipping into a dress that fits like a glove, but as you now know, that doesn't happen very often—*for anyone*. As I mentioned earlier, you are going to be asked to use your imagination a lot in this process, and it's important to understand whether you are someone who has the ability to do that or not. I think of it as a spectrum. On one end you might be a true creative who can really envision what the dress will look like after it's been altered, and on the other, you might really need to try it on to know how it will feel after it's been altered to fit you. Most women lie somewhere in the middle. But considering where you are on that spectrum will be helpful, because if you are someone who isn't great at envisioning, then you are going to want to find a dress that you love as-is without needing to make any changes to it.

Here are common things you are asked to envision:

- The dress fitting properly
- The dress being new and fresh and not the sample (It will be brighter, fuller, crisper, etc.)
- The dress at the correct length
- Things that can be done in alterations, like taking the volume out of the skirt or adding a sleeve, etc.

If you aren't quite sure what your imagination tolerance is, I encourage you to do the worksheet on our website that will help guide you.

Tip: See if you can find a dress in the same shape that fits, even if this is an evening gown instead of a wedding dress. Once you know you love a ball gown with a sweetheart neckline, you can better envision what an ill-fitting wedding dress sample will look like in your size.

GET INTO THE RIGHT HEADSPACE

It doesn't matter how beautiful, expensive, or special a dress is; if the woman putting it on isn't feeling good about herself, she's not going to love it—and you will be able to tell. This is why it's so important to understand the ways psychology can affect our style choices and also the way our outfits can impact our mood, level of confidence, and even how successfully we perform tasks throughout the day.

The psychology of style has been discussed in numerous articles, but the one I find most interesting is a 2012 University of Hertfordshire study led by Dr. Karen Pine, who discovered

Made-to-Measure vs. Made-to-Order vs. Off-the-Rack Dresses

There are two primary ways designers customize their wedding dress: made-to-measure and made-to-order. We are often asked what's the difference?

Made-to-measure dresses tend to be slightly more expensive and involve the designer taking upward of thirty measurements, creating a form based on your measurements, and then making the dress to the form.

Made-to-order dresses generally include just three measurements: your bust, waist, and hips. The designer creates the dress to fit the larger of the two and alters it later.

Off-the-rack dresses come as-is, meaning you try them on in the store in a specific size, buy that size, and if you need to make changes, you hire your own alterations person.

that many women choose clothing based on their emotional state. In the study, a majority of women (57 percent) said they were more likely to wear loose-fitting or "baggy" clothing when in a low mood or feeling depressed, whereas 62 percent of respondents said they'd be more likely to wear a favorite dress if feeling happy.[3] What does this have to do with wedding dress shopping? Well, everything.

This study highlights several key points:

- It's important to consider how your fashion choices influence the way others respond to you (including your maid of honor, who may have a negative knee-jerk reaction to a dress you love because it triggers something inside of her).
- Your emotional state can impact what you purchase.
- It's essential you do the work to get yourself in a good headspace before you go shopping for your dress.

I'd like to highlight some general tips to help you set yourself up for success. Note: I mention some of this in other areas of the book, but for quick reference, here's a short list:

- Buy a dress that you feel great wearing today, not for your ideal future self that is going to be thinner and more toned. That's too much pressure to put on yourself for a dress!
- Seriously consider who you bring with you for your dress-shopping journey. Having supportive and encouraging people by your side will make all the difference. If you are on the fence about including someone, go with your gut. You know deep down who will bring their own issues to the appointment and who won't.
- Take care of yourself before your shopping days. Drink enough water, get enough sleep, and eat nutritious foods that make you feel vibrant and healthy. I once tried to go register for gifts on a Sunday morning after a friend's birthday party the night before. Let's just say it wasn't my most productive moment, and I spent the whole time looking longingly at the beds, wanting to lie down!

Scan this QR code for additional resources from this chapter.

---

3 "News Release: Happiness: It's Not in the Jeans," University of Hertfordshire, March 2012, http://karenpine.com/wp-content/uploads/2012/03/PR-Happiness-its-not-in-the-jeans.pdf.

Chapter 5

PREP FOR PRICING

IT'S IMPORTANT TO CONSIDER your budget before you start shopping because it will be an indicator of which stores you should go to. Be aware that this isn't just the amount you will pay for your dress but also what you plan to spend on alterations, tax, and shipping, not to mention the fabulous accessories—shoes, jewelry, veil, etc.—you plan to wear on the big day.

If you're someone who feels uncomfortable talking about this subject, you're not alone. Most brides feel a little awkward when it comes to identifying a price point for their dress for a couple of reasons: They don't know what to expect when it comes to overall costs, and sharing a budget feels too revealing. Because most store consultants are paid on commission, brides worry that sharing the cap on what they can afford will negatively affect the service they get.

It's normal to have no idea where to start when creating a budget. Most brides I speak to don't know what to expect when it comes to overall costs because there is so little transparency about pricing. Not to worry. I am here to help!

THE LACK OF PRICE TRANSPARENCY

Fact: Most stores and designers won't list firm prices on their websites. If you're lucky, they'll show a range or highlight a "starting price," but more often than not, you won't be able to find anything at all. It's incredibly frustrating to the consumer but happens because of the wholesale/retail relationship between the designer and retailer. It works like this: The bridal designer creates a dress and then sells it to a boutique for a wholesale price. Then the boutique determines what their sale price will be, typically somewhere between 2.5 and 3 times the wholesale price. This is standard wholesale/retail procedure and happens with all types of goods but creates a challenge for brides trying to set an overall wedding budget.

There is nothing worse for either party than a bride going to a salon that isn't aligned with her budget. Not only will the bride leave disappointed, but it is also not ideal for the salon, which could have used that time on an appointment with a bride who is the right fit for them.

What can you do to make sure this doesn't happen and also set up a reasonable and comfortable budget for yourself? Here are my suggestions:

- Call the stores you are interested in visiting and ask about their price range before booking an appointment. If their answer is vague, don't be afraid to dig deeper. For example, if your budget is $5,000 and they say, "Our starting price point is $3,000 and goes up to $20,000," I would ask what the average price is and also how many dresses they have that are under $5,000 so you can decide if it's worth your time to go to that store.
- Do some online sleuthing on sites that sell used wedding dresses because they often list the original dress price.
- Read articles dedicated to wedding dress pricing from bridal magazines and websites.
- Refer to my Designer Directory on the website.

After doing all that, once you are at the appointment, always be honest with the consultant about your budget. If you are concerned about sharing a small number, remember that *every* bride has a budget, and the consultant would much rather you tell them up-front so they can show you options that will work. Don't waste time by trying on things you can't afford. I have worked with some of the wealthiest families in the world, and I can assure you that *everyone* has a budget they feel comfortable with. Setting a range is normal, and I never see it as what someone can afford but rather as what someone is *willing* to spend.

How much do women actually spend?

While there is no finite number, most experts say that wedding fashion (for both the bride and groom) should account for 10 percent of the overall wedding budget. A recent *Brides* magazine study revealed that the average bride in America spends $2,439 on her wedding dress. But each bride will have her own way of identifying her number. The key is to figure out what works for you and then be realistic about what is available at your price point.

BREAKING DOWN YOUR DRESS BUDGET

Earlier in this chapter, I mentioned that your budget should not only account for the dress but also other costs you can expect to encounter. Let's break these down now.

Fittings

We are going to get into the intricacies of fittings in Chapter 9, but I wanted to mention them here because they do add to the overall cost of the dress. I'm sure it won't come as a surprise that every designer and boutique has a different way of charging for fittings. Sometimes it's a flat fee, sometimes it's a percentage of the price of the dress, and sometimes it's a number based on the amount of work necessary.

Altering a wedding dress is a true craft and requires someone who knows what they are doing. *Please* do not choose someone only because they are the "cheapest" option. I have heard too many stories from brides who tried to save a few dollars only to have their dresses fit poorly or even be ruined.

As a real-life example, in New York City the standard starting price point for fittings for a designer dress is about $700 and goes up from there. However, it can be a few hundred dollars cheaper in other parts of the country. Brides typically have a total of three fittings, so when you divide it up and consider the amount of work each fitting requires, the cost starts to make more sense.

Everything Else

When you consider your budget, don't forget these items, which we will discuss further in later chapters:

- **Accessories and undergarments:** Other things you need to factor in are shoes, undergarments, and accessories. These can cost anywhere from a few hundred dollars to a few thousand.
- **Shipping and sales tax:** I've grouped these two items together because currently in the US when a dress is shipped to a state where a brand does not have a store or representation, the sales tax isn't charged, but the shipping cost is. You should check with the store and state for more information.
- **Cleaning and preserving your dress:** Done right, this is expensive and can add an extra $1,000-plus to your budget. When I got married, I had this fantasy that my theoretical daughter would someday wear my wedding dress. Now that I have her and know her, I think this is *highly* unlikely! But at least she will have the option someday.

  If you do decide to preserve it, don't just pick the first person you find or the cheapest. Wedding dresses should be cleaned and preserved by experts, and it is important to speak to the store where you purchased the dress or other customers (preferably someone you know) to make sure you are in good hands. Take photos of your dress before you hand it over and take care to note any stains, tears, and discolorations. I have a colleague who had two wedding dresses cleaned by a vendor with a beautiful website and loads of "great" reviews, only to be handed a dress with a tear and a large stain and another dress with the breast pads glaring through the dress, making them look like two bleach stains.

Spending Tracker
DATE
DESCRIPTION
AMOUNT
CASH
CARD

FINDING A DRESS THAT FITS *YOUR* BUDGET

Let's talk about how to locate your dream dress without slipping out of your budget.

Wedding dresses can range in price anywhere from $1,000–$500,000 (or more), but there really are three main groupings to consider: under $3,000; $3,000–$6,000; and $6,000 and above.

For a comprehensive list of designers by price point, scan the QR code at the end of the chapter.

I must mention that it's quite common for designers to have a range of prices and fall into two pricing categories. For example, Oscar de la Renta may have $5,000 dresses as well as dresses that are well over $20,000 (and Amal Clooney's was more than $300,000). So when calling the stores, you may want to ask the average price of a dress so you can get a sense for where they are on the spectrum.

While you will always pay more for top design-house talent, it really comes down to who the designer is, what the dress is made of, and how long it took to make. Special fabrics like French lace and silk are gorgeous but also carry heavy price tags. The same is true for materials like Swarovski crystals and time- and talent-heavy details, like intricate beading, boning, and embroidery.

Working with a Smaller Budget

A smaller budget doesn't mean you can't wear a dress you love; it just means that you will need to prioritize your "must-haves" and your "nice-to-haves" the same way you will when planning the rest of your wedding. Personally, I absolutely love fabrics, so when I was getting married, I knew I wanted a dress that was made of exquisite silk. I've spoken with other brides who don't care that much about fabrics, but they want to be sure their dress has lace or some other detail. Unless you are in the very top range of budgets (I'm talking $10,000-plus), you are going to have to prioritize (or shop secondhand). It's normal, and you're in very good company, I promise.

Here's my rule of thumb: The smaller the budget, the simpler the dress. Focus on uncomplicated designs and personalize them with gorgeous accessories. Dresses in this category can be found off-the-rack (pre-made in a range of sizes and available in stores), on pre-owned dress websites, and even in vintage shops. I know one bride who found a gorgeous gown on a charity shop website for $550.

WHAT TO EXPECT IN TERMS OF PRICING

There are several factors that go into determining the price of a wedding dress, and as I mentioned above, the key is to determine what is important to you. Below are the main factors to help you make an educated decision.

The designer who makes it: How important is a designer's name to you? Are you someone who enjoys being able to say that your outfit was made by a high-profile designer? Or maybe you prefer to find small, unknown designers who are really cool. Or maybe it doesn't matter to you at all so long as you love the dress. This question is something to think about because it's going to influence what you can get for the money. It comes as no surprise that, generally, the bigger the designer's name is the more expensive the dress will be. If you are on a budget, a great way to go can be finding a small designer who's just starting out (but has a proven track record and good references). You can save a lot by not having a big designer name attached to your dress.

The quality of the fabric used: This one gets a little tricky, because you can technically get any of these fabrics at any price point. However, the quality of the materials is most likely going to be different (i.e., polyester satin vs. silk satin). I should start by explaining what determines the quality of fabric. Simply put, it's the materials that are used to make it. The lower-quality and cheaper fabrics have little (if any) natural fibers in them. Higher-quality fabrics are mostly (if not entirely) made up of all-natural fibers, which are of course more expensive to produce. There are also blends, and the same rule typically applies. For example, a silk faille with a little stretch to it is still a high-quality fabric.

You can find a lace dress at the $1,000–$3,000 price point, and it will be made of lace that's polyester. A lace dress in the $6,000-plus category, however, will have a finer lace made of natural fibers such as cotton, silk, or even linen. The finest laces of all come from Italy and France and are made by a handful of companies, like Solstiss. Of course, there are exceptions to every rule, and I can tell you there are definitely outliers to this list. Can you find a simple silk dress at the $1,000–$3,000 price point? Most definitely, but probably not from a top designer who makes their dresses to order.

How much fabric is required: This is pretty self-explanatory, but regardless of the price of the fabric, the more fabric that's needed, the more expensive the dress is to produce.

The details and embellishments: Again, my advice to brides on a budget looking for a high-quality dress is always to keep it simple. Lace, embroidery, and beading all add to the cost of production and are going to raise the price of the gown. The pricing for these items is just like it is for fabrics: The higher-quality goods are made with better materials and are sometimes made by hand. It's all about your priorities. You can find an all-lace dress from a mid-priced designer that is the same price as a simple dress from a top designer.

How and where it's made: Designers in the lower price ranges often have their dresses mass-produced overseas. Just like in ready-to-wear clothing, this keeps the costs down. Conversely, most of the top designers make the dresses to order and can therefore often do it in the country where they are located. This allows them to stay on top of quality control, production timelines, and shipping needs. It's definitely more expensive, but you also get a higher-quality product.

Average Costs of Fabrics

This list of fabrics provides an overview of the most common cost scenarios. Yes, you may be able to find some of the higher-quality fabrics in the lower ranges, but those will be outliers.

Under $3,000	$3,000–$6,000	$6,000+
Charmeuse	Charmeuse	Anything from the previous columns
Chiffon	Chiffon	Duchesse satin
Crêpe	Crêpe	Mikado/Zibeline
Dupioni	Damask	Moiré
Polyester	Dupioni	Organza
Rayon	Georgette	Silk faille
	Lace	Silk gazar
	Mikado/Zibeline	Silk satin
	Polyester	Silk taffeta
	Rayon	
	Satin	
	Shantung	
	Silk	
	Swiss dot (point d'esprit)	
	Taffeta	
	Tulle	
	Voile	

Now that you have a budget and understand some of the cost parameters, let's talk about how to set you up for dress success!

Scan this QR code for additional resources from this chapter.

Chapter 6

PLAN LIKE A PRO

AS WITH MOST THINGS, when it comes to finding your dress, your success often depends on having an effective strategy. One of the most common questions we are asked is when you should start shopping for your wedding dress. The quick answer and best practice is nine to twelve months before your wedding and only *after* you have the date and location set. (If you do it before you know the details, it will be inefficient because the best dress for you is highly influenced by the venue and season.) With that said, I can tell you that regardless of your timeline, there is a dress out there for you.

Below are a few things to consider when planning the shopping day of your dreams.

KNOW WHERE TO LOOK

Remember our discussion about identifying your top list of designers? Now it's time to find out where their dresses are sold. The best way to do this is to pull up the designer's website and take a look at their stockists (the retailers that carry their dresses). This is where you will find all of the stores and boutiques that carry their designs. Now, if you live in New York City (the wedding dress capital of the world), you will likely find loads of shops in close proximity to one another, but that is not the case in other cities and smaller towns, so it pays to do your research.

KNOW THYSELF (AND STAY TRUE TO YOU!)

So much in this book comes back to this core concept, but it's especially true when shopping for your dress. Not only do you need to know the kinds of designs you are looking for, but you also need to think about *how* you like to shop, your stamina, and the number of options you personally need to see before making a decision. Equally important is knowing your point of overwhelm and steering clear of it.

Shopping in New York

If you *do* have a little extra in your budget and want to use it to come to New York City for your shopping, I highly recommend it—if you do it right, you'll have a blast! Make sure you plan in advance, do your research, and set up your appointments well ahead of time (at least eight weeks) to guarantee you see everything you want to see. If you have more questions about it, you can find our New York Shopping Guide on our website.

For example, I have some clients who hate to shop and really can't imagine going to six different stores in a day (or even six in total). Others need to see *everything* before deciding and want me to take them to *every store* that has potential options for them. You might be surprised to hear that I love working with both, mainly because they know who they are and they let me know how to best support them from the very beginning. This sets everyone up for success and makes for a much smoother shopping process.

Think about how many stores you can tolerate in a day and stick to that number. On the first day you shop, I personally recommend going to at least three appointments. This will speed up the learning curve because you will see dresses back-to-back and you will get into a groove. It can be hard to remember every dress, so doing it this way, while they are fresh in your mind, is important. Don't forget to take photos from every angle and in the best lighting available.

IDENTIFYING YOUR DECISION-MAKING STYLE

This isn't something that many people give a lot of thought to, but it's *so* important. You don't necessarily have to do it before you start shopping, but it would be helpful to do it early on in the process as it will save you a lot of time.

While they might have an idea of what they are looking for, many women worry that they aren't going to find a dress that they love, and it's common for people to say, "Don't worry; you will just know." This is true for *some* lucky brides but not all, or even *most*, of them! The truth is brides are having a harder time than ever before when it comes to finding their wedding dress thanks to thousands of options, a constant stream of gorgeous photos on social media, and knowledge of what their friends—and friends' friends—wore down the aisle. Add on the opinions of the friends, family, and future in-laws, and the shopping experience can feel pretty overwhelming. Understanding how you make decisions will not only help you navigate through a stream of never-ending options but also give you the confidence to trust yourself when you think you have found *the one*.

Are you a Maximizer or a Satisficer?

There are a lot of different opinions out there on how the cognitive process works when we make decisions. To my mind, the most relevant in terms of selecting a wedding dress is the difference between the cognitive styles of **Maximizers** and **Satisficers.**

Here is how Wikipedia defines them:

Maximizing is a style of decision making characterized by seeking the best option by exhaustively searching through alternatives. It has three major components: having high standards, being willing to search for alternatives, and having difficulty making decisions.

Satisficing, on the other hand, blends the traits of *satisfying* and *sufficing*. This is when individuals evaluate options until they find one that is "good enough." They select the first option that meets a given need or the option that seems to address most needs, rather than the "optimal" solution.

I am a Maximizer through-and-through. In fact, not knowing the right term for it, I've called myself an "Agonizer" for years. One great example of this was when I was searching for my dress. I had to see every possible option to be able to make a decision. I tried on hundreds of dresses and drove everyone insane. And thank goodness, because it led me to start The Stylish Bride®, a business that I've loved for more than twenty years, where I've been fortunate enough to help many brides make the right decisions for themselves.

Funnily enough, this quality (which can drive me completely crazy) is probably what makes me good at my job. My clients know that if I am considering all the options for them, they don't need to! But honestly, sometimes it can be excruciating to be in my head weighing all the pros and cons of everything. Just ask my husband, who has been witness to it since 1999!

Let's look at how these two decision-making styles play out in the search for the perfect wedding dress.

Let's start with the **Maximizers**, as they are near and dear to my heart. If you know that you are a Maximizer, you are going to want to give yourself plenty of time for your dress search because we both know that you will want to see everything out there and probably go back again once (if not multiple times) to see your favorites before making a final decision.

I've found that my Maximizer clients don't cry when they put on *the* dress that they ultimately select. They smile, they stare at it, and they keep it on longer than others, but they aren't typically emotional because they won't really know that it's the one until they think about it for a while and compare it to other options.

For you Maximizers, I think it's a good idea to tell the consultants helping you in the stores that you are someone who needs to take their time making a decision. That way they know that you aren't purchasing a dress the first time you try it on and that they will probably see you again.

Now, if you are a **Satisficer**, lucky you! It's going to be a much easier process. My Satisficer clients are typically the ones that do cry (or at least know) when they find their dream dress. We often go to a few appointments and then end up going back to the favorite dress and buying it. Sometimes they even want to cancel the other appointments because they don't feel they need to try more on.

What's amazing about these brides is that they typically have no regrets and feel totally satisfied with their choice. I even had one client buy the second dress she tried on. That same day! As a Maximizer, I was like, "Are you *sure*?" She smiled and said, "Yep! Let's do it and go to lunch!" I was a little worried, but you know what? She loved it! Side note: I always recommend sleeping on it for a night before pulling out your credit card, but some brides just know and know themselves enough to say yes right then and there.

With that said, I've also had brides who do that (despite my advice otherwise) and wake up the next day, freak out, and regret their decision. I've also had brides who presented as Satisficers but were really just impulsive. These ladies *thought* they found the one and, after sleeping on it, changed their minds and selected something else. Thank goodness they hadn't already purchased the dress and weren't stuck with an impulse buy. This type of change of heart happens all the time and for different reasons, including showing it to someone who doesn't love it, studying the pictures and changing their mind about it, or just a good old-fashioned dose of self-doubt.

Whatever happens, I encourage you to take a step back and think about it for a day or two. This can help you avoid making a costly mistake—because remember, the 50 percent deposit is non-refundable.

If you are unsure where you fall on this spectrum (or you fall somewhere in the middle), I encourage you to go to at least a few appointments, even if you find something you like at the first one. You can also take our quiz on our website to help you identify your style.

TWO BRIDES DRESS SHOPPING

How do you navigate this process if you and your partner are both women? If you both want to wear a dress, you're most likely wondering, *Do we shop separately or together? If separately, who goes first?*

The first question about shopping together or separately is part personal preference and part logistics. In order to figure this out, I'd start by deciding if you are more traditional and prefer to be surprised at the altar or at your first-look photos when it comes to seeing your partner. If so, then you are going to want to shop at different times. If that isn't the case and you are excited to participate in the process together, I'd suggest not doing two appointments at the same time in a salon. First off, this is going to be hard to schedule. Secondly, I truly feel that you should each have your moment to focus solely on your own bridal look. It is a lot of work

Lessons from a Real Bride

A Satisficer through-and-through, Stephanie was going to be an easy client. She knew what she liked and what she didn't. She had a clear vision of what she wanted to wear and the details that really felt like *her*. We had a smooth and fun day of dress shopping, and all was going well.

Then, at our last appointment, she spontaneously tried on a dress that was way outside of her style profile. I always think it's great to do that and explore all of the options, and I didn't think twice about having a little fun by having her try on a tulle ball gown. But then, she loved it. I mean *really* fell in love with it, so much so that she said that was it! Now, let me just say that it was a beautiful dress and really looked great on her, but it was just SO different from what she wanted.

Anyway, she surprised me when she said that she was ready to order the dress, right then and there. I told her that she should take some time to think about it, sleep on it, and see how she felt. But she was adamant that it was the *one* and she didn't need to. So, she took measurements, signed the contract, and put down her 50 percent deposit.

The next day, I got a frantic call from her that she'd made a mistake and no longer wanted the dress! She said she had gotten swept up in the drama and romance of it and realized that it wasn't really her.

Because of my long-standing relationship with the designer, they kindly refunded her deposit (which they were not required to do in the contract!), and we took a few days to regroup. We ended up going back to one of the first stores we visited, now with a whole new perspective, and decided on a totally different dress. In the end it all worked out, but she could have saved herself—and me—a few gray hairs if she had slept on it!

to really consider each dress and how you feel wearing it. It can be hard to focus if you are also considering what your partner is feeling and wearing.

Now, the hard part: deciding who will go first. Hopefully, you will know what is right for you, but if you need a little help, consider the following things:

1. Does one of you take longer to make decisions? If so, that person should go first.
2. Do either of you hate shopping? If so, they should go second so they can benefit from the knowledge gained from the other's experience.
3. Does one of you care about this much more than the other? If so, start with the one who cares most.

WHEN TO SHOP

Once you have a plan, you'll need to book your appointments. Whenever possible, shop on a weekday. Not only will it be easier to schedule, but it will also be a calmer atmosphere, and you will receive more one-on-one attention. Some salons even have longer weekday appointments than those on a weekend.

While you *can* have a great experience on a Saturday, there's no getting around the fact that it's the most crowded and chaotic day of the week to shop. This lends itself to a number of challenges—from the longer advanced booking (Saturdays are usually reserved six weeks or more ahead of time) and having to compete with other brides to try on dresses to working with exhausted consultants who have been pulled from one dressing room to another all day, often without a break or a bite to eat.

You can only imagine what that means for the bride who arrives late in the afternoon. The poor consultant may be completely dedicated to giving you the best experience they can, but have you ever been at your best when feeling exhausted and hungry? I didn't think so. While it might sound fun to help brides find their dream dress, I can tell you firsthand it's one of the most demanding and emotional jobs in the industry.

I remember when I worked in a bridal dress boutique on Saturdays. After dozens of ups and downs catering to brides with different personalities, needs, desires, and reactions, I used to go home and take a long hot bath (because my body was so sore), have a huge martini (which helped a great deal), and collapse onto my bed. I could barely hold a conversation with my husband (because of exhaustion, not the martini, for those wondering!).

That said, if you must book on a Saturday, get in there as early as possible. In fact, if you can get the first appointment time of the day, snatch it up like the golden ticket it is. The shop will feel more serene, and the consultants are much more likely to be fresh and focused.

TSB

The Stylish Bride

Caroline's Wedding Dress
Shopping Itinerary

Thursday, August 17th, 2023

9:30 a.m	SPINA Bride	132 10th Ave
11:00 a.m	Lee Petra Grebenau	176 MacDougal St
12:30 p.m	Monique Lhuillier	818 Madison Ave @ 69th
1:30 p.m	Quick Bite Bel Ami Cafe	30 E. 68th
1:45 p.m	Elie Saab	860 Madison Ave @ 70th
3:15 p.m	Romona Keveza	1 Rockefeller Plaza, PH
4:30 p.m	Reem Acra	501 5th Ave Fl 2
5:30 p.m	Approx End.	

Friday, August 18th, 2023

10:00 a.m	Oscar De La Renta Bridal	772 Madison @ 66th
10:45 a.m	Oscar De La Renta RTW	772 Madison @ 66th
11:30 a.m	Monique Lhuillier RTW	818 Madison Ave @ 69th
12:15 p.m	Elie Saab RTW	860 Madison Ave @ 70th
1:30 p.m	Carolina Herrera	954 Madison Ave @ 75th
2:30 p.m	Approx End.	

SCHEDULING YOUR APPOINTMENTS

Now that you have decided when and where you are going, it's time to make your bookings. I have to tell you that scheduling appointments for our clients is the bane of our existence. It's *complicated*! In fact, at The Stylish Bride, we hired a dedicated person to handle the gargantuan task of planning, scheduling, and managing appointments for our clients because it's such a beast of a job.

Here is what you will find:

Opening times: Many stores are closed on Sunday. Some are closed Sunday and Monday, others on Tuesday or Wednesday. It's maddening. But if you're trying to select the best day to shop, Thursday and Friday are typically safe bets.

Available appointment times: Every store has different hours and appointment times. For example, some open at 9:30 AM, some at 10:00 AM, and still others at 10:15 AM. Some take a lunch break for the whole store, while others stagger their staff lunches. If that's not frustrating enough, all of this is subject to change at any time.

Length of the appointment: Appointment length varies not only by salon but also by the day in some cases. As I mentioned above, some salons may offer an hour-and-a-half appointment on weekdays but only an hour on the weekend. Others will allow the same amount of time each day. Be sure to ask so that you know how much time to allot for each one.

Travel time: Being late to an appointment is never a good idea as there is not a lot of flexibility when it comes to extending appointment times. Besides, even *thinking* you might be late will add an extra layer of stress to your experience, so make sure you give yourself enough time to get from salon A to salon B without having to break a sweat. Look up traffic reports and train times and add fifteen minutes extra to the suggested commuting time to allow for any unforeseen delays. Trust me—there will come a time when you'll thank me for this.

How to book the appointment: This is another area where the stores vary. Some use online booking systems, whereas others require a telephone call. I'm old-school in this way and think calling is a better way to go because you can ask questions, request a specific consultant, and tell them critical information like any sizing challenges you face or budget parameters you have. You can also confirm that a dress you are dying to try on will be there for the appointment, and if it won't be, ask for it to be brought in for you. Most salons will follow up with an email that details procedural guidelines and what you can expect.

What to prepare: At the beginning of the appointment, the consultant will usually ask you a few questions about your wedding (date, location, vibe) and what you are looking for in terms of your dress. This is your moment to communicate all of your thoughts into a short synopsis to help them guide you. Many brides find it difficult to communicate and ask me to do the talking.

Monique Lhuillier

But don't worry if you don't know the lingo. Whip out your Bridal Style Blueprint, and everything you need to tell them is right there. Add to that photos of any dresses you have tried on that you love or specifically want to see from their collection, and you're off to the races.

WHAT TO BRING WITH YOU

My clients often ask me what they need to bring with them to try on dresses, and really, the short answer is *nothing*. However, there are a few things that will make the process run more smoothly and offer you more flexibility and support. You can find my favorite "extras" below and decide which ones are right for you. I've also put together a checklist for you on our website with a link to our Amazon shop where you can purchase these items.

Shoes: While most salons generally have shoes in various sizes for clients to use during appointments, this isn't always the case. And, if the salon is packed, you might be waiting awhile (particularly if you wear a common shoe size). If you want to be safe (or have a specific heel height in mind), I suggest you bring a pair with you that are easy to slide on and off.

Underwear: First of all, wear them. If you aren't someone who wears underwear on a regular basis, make sure you do for these appointments. You do not want to be the bride being sent out to buy undies (because they *will* send you out to get some).

And keep in mind that nude undies are the best option for wedding dress shopping. Darker colors can be seen under the dresses and are incredibly distracting in real life and photos. You would be shocked how many brides never think of this and have bright purple undies showing through in their shopping photos. It's actually quite funny.

Shapewear: Contrary to what you might think, I'm a big proponent of *not* wearing shapewear on your wedding day. I think they are torture devices that can make you feel hotter and more uncomfortable! That said, they can be extremely helpful while wedding dress shopping for two reasons: (1) they provide coverage for brides who are modest, and (2) they make it easier to get in and out of a dress that is too small.

Bras: There are two categories of dresses: those that have built-in bust support and those that don't. If you aren't particularly busty, you won't need extra support. But if you *are*, you're going to want to give yourself some lift so you can really see what the dresses will look like. In my experience, strapless bras tend to be pretty worthless, so I suggest bringing bust-lift tape or a sticky bra instead.

Snacks and water: This is where the mother in me comes out. There is nothing worse than shopping when you are hangry or low energy. I make sure to keep almonds and a PowerBar in my bag. The New York salons I visit on a daily basis have water on hand, but others may not, so go prepared!

Phone charger: We know by now that photos are critical to the shopping process, and you don't want to run out of juice.

Hair tie: It's great to be able to see your hair pulled back with the dress on. A hair tie is also helpful should you be interested in trying on a veil.

Sample Size Solution: I designed this product to modify a wedding dress sample so that any bride—*regardless of their shape or size*—can try it on. By using the tools included you will be able to see more clearly how a dress will fit your shape and to avoid a gaping hole in the back when it doesn't zip up. (See pages 70 and 71 for more details on this kit.)

WHO TO BRING WITH YOU

I want to start by saying that I think most people have the best intentions. Over the years I've pretty much seen it all when it comes to shopping companions and have often been surprised at how an opinionated, boisterous friend can be supportive and objective during appointments. But I've also seen it go the other way and watched as a subtle comment or a facial expression can totally change how a bride feels in a dress. So as you can imagine, who you bring with you is a critical piece of the experience and can make or break your day.

I not only advise you to carefully select whom you invite but also recommend that you have no more than two people with you. I know it's tempting to bring your whole gang, because what could be more fun than a day with your best girlfriends and family? The final head count depends on your individual circumstances, but I mean it when I say that this is one time that the more is not the merrier.

How to Make It Special

- Pop the champagne!
- Brunch or lunch is a must
- Write it down
- Hire a photographer

If you have to narrow your list down, it can be really hard to select who to bring. You want to make sure loved ones don't feel excluded, but you also want to have the experience that is right for you and sets you up for success. On the website I have included a list of questions that can help you navigate these tricky waters, but the bottom line is that you want to surround yourself with people that are supportive, unbiased, and able to let you decide before they give an opinion.

However, every once in a while when I shop with a client who has brought along a large group, I'll often give them some gentle advice on how they can participate in a productive way. These are great things to share with whomever you bring:

1. Don't voice your opinion on the dress before the bride does. It's incredibly important that she has the space and freedom to consider the dress and voice her thoughts first.
2. Express your feelings when asked but do so in a constructive way. For example, instead of saying, "I hate it," try, "I prefer the particular detail on the last one," or something along those lines.
3. Don't fall in love with a dress and compare all others to it if the bride doesn't love it as well.
4. Never ever start a sentence with "For my wedding, I . . ." It's not your wedding! As fun as it is to reminisce, the comparison is not helpful for the bride.

How do you handle those who aren't up to the task?

Let's say that you have asked yourself the tough questions and realized that your super-practical sister might not be the right person to take shopping with you. How do you break this to her without ruining the relationship? Simple—tell her that you want to try things on first and then take her along to select the veil or to the final dress fitting.

STRATEGIC PLANNING

I am very strategic in how I set up wedding dress shopping days for clients. In addition to the intricacies of the scheduling, there is a whole master plan behind how I choose the order that we go in. There is a huge learning curve in trying on wedding dresses, so here is my advice on how to structure your appointments:

- **The first appointment:** Make this appointment at a store that has a wide selection but is not overwhelming. In New York, it is often a designer's boutique rather than a multi-vendor store so that you can try different shapes and fabrics, but you don't have to remember the differences between designers' styles. This appointment is for you to start shaping the big concept of what you like.
- **The second and third appointments:** By now, you are still learning, but you are not a complete novice. I like to book these at stores where you can focus on particular designers you are interested in, but who are not your favorites. You are now getting familiar with the intricacies of wedding dresses and

The Difference Between a Salon and a Designer Boutique

If you're visiting a traditional bridal salon, you will have an opportunity to try on a curated selection of dresses from different designers, whereas a designer's boutique will carry the full collection only from a particular designer.

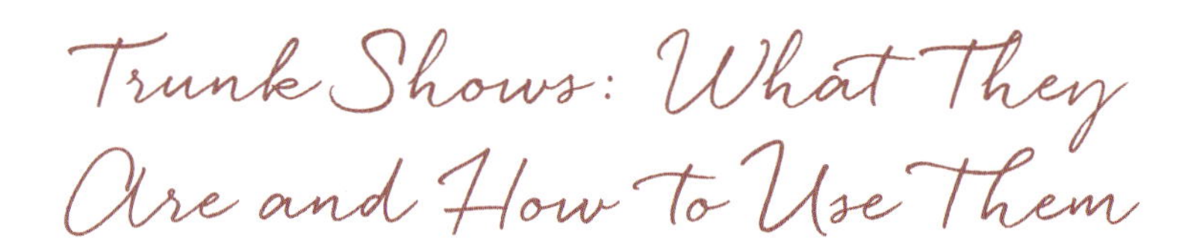

Trunk Shows: What They Are and How to Use Them

More than ever before, trunk shows have become a crucial part of a bride-to-be's dress search. The problem is that brides don't know what they are or how to navigate them. Here is a little cheat sheet to help you.

What is a trunk show, exactly?

It's when a designer (or their sales representative) travels to different stores around the country or the world, bringing their latest collection in its entirety for brides to try on. Since it often takes six months or more for the dresses off the runway to arrive in the stores, a trunk show gives you access to the newest styles.

Why are trunk shows special?

Put simply, trunk shows are a showcase for a designer's collection, including their newest designs. This is exciting as most bridal salons only carry a few styles from each designer in their permanent collection. Also, since the designer or their representative will be present, they can give their expert opinion on the gown and may also be able to make custom changes to a dress—something many designers won't do otherwise. But wait, it gets even better. Most stores will offer brides incentives for any purchase made during a trunk show, such as a 10 percent discount or a free veil.

How do I find out when trunk shows are happening?

Most designers and bridal salons will have trunk show dates and details on their websites. Some will also inform brides via social media. Trunk shows are planned *way* in advance, and they get booked up very quickly, so I advise that you check early and often!

Are there any disadvantages to trunk shows?

You won't be able to go back and see the dress again because at the end of the weekend, the dresses jet off to their next city. So if you are not ready to purchase a dress that day (understandable with such a big decision), take lots of photos and videos if you really love it.

Any special tips?

Yes. Because designers can't travel with every dress they've made, the one you want may not have been on the list or may have been pulled for a photoshoot. So if there is a specific dress you have your eye on, call the store in advance and make sure it will be there. If it won't be, they can often bring it with them specifically for you.

the totally different vocabulary used. Your focus should be on identifying elements you like and don't like and starting to home in on the shape and fabric you like the most. I would suggest making these two appointments on the same day as the first, so you keep the momentum going.

- **Appointment four:** At this point in the shopping process you've got a really strong foundation, and it's time to drill down on the particular dresses you love. When I'm structuring a fourth shopping appointment, I line up a favorite designer or one that I think will be a great fit for the client's style profile. You know enough about dresses to be able to identify what you like, and you are ready to get serious.
- **Appointment five:** I often make this a store that carries multiple designers so you can see a lot of different styles and confirm what you are thinking thus far. It's great to be able to go into these appointments with the clear vision you have gotten from the previous appointments, and I encourage you to show the consultants what you loved from those stores. Because the selection is so wide, this information will really help the consultant be effective and suggest dresses that are similar to the ones you already love.

Scan this QR code for additional resources from this chapter.

EMILIA WICKSTEAD
EMILIA WICKSTEAD

Chapter 7

THE APPOINTMENTS (FINALLY!)

SO, YOU HAVE CHOSEN your stores, have made your appointments, and are ready to start trying on dresses. This is a huge step in your wedding planning journey, and it's completely normal to feel both excited and overwhelmed. The good news is that you are set up for dress success because you have taken the time to plan and prepare by *thoughtfully* doing your Bridal Style Blueprint; identifying what kind of decision-maker you are; equipping yourself with the basics of dress shapes, fabrics, and details; and strategically planning your shopping experience. You are so far ahead of the game that it's time to have some fun!

FIRST UP

Your shopping day is finally here, and all your hard work and planning has paid off. YAY! A word of advice from someone who has been to thousands of wedding dress shopping appointments: Go in with an open mind. I can't tell you the number of times a client of mine has ended up with the exact thing they said they didn't want!

With that said, at the beginning of the day, I encourage my clients to try on a range of shapes and styles, including ones they think they don't want, just to make sure. So while I am not suggesting you waste time by trying on a beaded dress if you hate sparkle, do sample several different shapes, necklines, and fabrics just to make sure. Who knows—you might surprise yourself. I'll give you an example:

I once worked with a bride who had been dreaming about a strapless ball gown "from the age of seven" and was very clear that she only wanted to try on dresses that fit her idea of the perfect dress. I suggested we spend the first day trying on several shapes, but she was unconvinced, so we went from salon to salon trying on different versions of the same look. Though she liked some more than others, she didn't *love* any of them, and at the end of the day, she confessed that she felt "disappointed and confused" by the fact that her theoretical dream dress didn't look or feel as perfect as she had hoped.

The next day, I suggested that we try on several different shapes, even those with elements she swore she "could never" wear (in her case, a slim skirt). To her surprise, she found a dress that looked stunning and made her feel beautiful—with, you guessed it, a slim skirt!

This scene has played out in my career many times. Brides often forget that wedding dresses fit differently than ready-to-wear, and the only real way to know how a dress will look on you is to try it on! This is why I strongly encourage you to allow yourself to step out of your comfort zone and spend the first appointment trying on lots of different styles and shapes until you narrow down the one or two you love most and then use them as a baseline for the rest of your appointments.

THE SALES CONSULTANT'S JOB

I'd like to take a minute to go over what a bridal salon consultant does—*and doesn't do*—because their responsibilities are probably different than those of any other salesperson you have worked with before.

Put simply, a consultant's job is to help you navigate the shopping experience by providing a high level of expertise in various shapes and designs to curate a dress selection that keeps your vision in mind. They should also introduce you to a few looks similar to your core style that you may not have considered (or even known about).

While some salespeople might bring that fun, sparkly "best friend" energy you see in the movies, many will not—and that's OK! Just as the consultant needs to keep your preferences in mind, it's important for you to remember that they are professionals working with multiple brides, often in high-stress situations, with a lot on their plates. It's far more important they understand your aesthetic and make you feel comfortable than whether or not they get excited when you look great in your dress.

I have the highest respect for the bridal consultants we work with on a regular basis and see them as our partners in finding our clients the best dresses for them. When you get a great consultant, the shopping experience is different, and you are confident you are in good hands.

How to Fire a Consultant

Feeling out of sync with a consultant? Not sure that they get you or are listening to what you want? It's uncommon, but it happens. The best way to handle this is to simply finish the appointment, call the store afterwards, and speak to the manager. Unless something truly unprofessional happened, avoid going into a long list of reasons you don't want to work with the person and simply say you didn't feel a connection and would like to book an appointment with someone else. The store would much rather you come back than go elsewhere.

A good consultant wants both the positive and negative feedback. I've worked with many brides who feel uncomfortable telling the consultant when they don't like a dress. But this is actually exactly what they want you to do (in a kind way, of course) because it helps them help you. I work with one consultant who always says to the bride, "You won't hurt my feelings; I didn't design it," and another who says, "The dresses don't have feelings, so tell me what you think." Remember, your goal is the same: to find a dress that you love.

TAKE PHOTOS!

When I first started my business in the early aughts, cell phones didn't have cameras and most bridal salons forbade taking photos because they were afraid you were going to take them to a seamstress and have the dress copied. This began to change thanks to smartphone technology and the subsequent "influencer age." It's a good thing, too, because photos are probably the single most effective tool in your wedding dress search. Nowadays, any shop that wants to stay competitive allows a bride to record her experience.

I applaud this shift since I am a huge fan of photographing *everything*, and let's be real: Most brides are not looking to go through the hassle of finding a seamstress to try and create a dress from a few phone photos. Not only does taking pictures allow you to see the dress from different angles, but it's also a fantastic way to make side-by-side comparisons between dresses. This will help you decide between two dresses you love as well as make it easier to identify (and communicate) elements you don't like so that you can find your dream dress a lot faster.

Every time we are with clients, we use a collage app that allows you to upload two, three, or even four photos next to each other so you can compare and contrast different dresses. It is SO helpful and facilitates the decision making exponentially.

When photographing a dress, here are some things to consider:

- Take at least one photo of every dress you try on (even the ones you don't like) so that you have a record of them. It can be helpful information in the future.
- For the dresses that are contenders, make sure you photograph all angles in full-length shots. You want to see the whole dress from the front, back, and both sides.
- Take close-up shots of the details so you can remember the intricacies of the design.
- Ask the consultant where the best angle is for photos because I guarantee you they know. You want to make sure the area where you are taking the photos is well-lit and, if possible, in natural light. Fabrics, sheerness, and colors are often different in natural light, and it's imperative to know that before buying.
- Try to stand in the same position when you take photos so it's easier to compare them when you put them side by side.

Use video to your advantage.

For the dresses you *really* love, taking a video of you walking in the dress is a fantastic way to capture the movement of the dress and get a sense of what you will need to have done during your alterations.

FUNCTIONALITY: PREVIEW VERSUS PERFORMANCE

Understanding the difference between how a dress looks in the store and how it will work on your wedding day is one of the most important considerations you will make when choosing your dress. Let me explain. In the store, you are standing on a pedestal, in fantastic lighting and a temperature-controlled environment. Everything is designed for your comfort and to highlight the dress in an optimum setting. This, of course, will be very different from your wedding day, when the temperature and natural elements like wind, rain, and terrain can really impact the functionality, practicality, and appropriateness of the dress itself.

To give you an example of what I mean, I am currently working with a bride who is getting married on the top of Aspen Mountain in Colorado, and one of the things we talk about a lot when she is trying on dresses is how it's going to look and react in that environment. We are looking for something that's going to have a beautiful, flowing fabric so that when the train is caught by the wind the motion can be captured in photos.

This brings me to the subject of the length of the train. Many times in the store, brides talk about wanting it to be longer and wanting a grand train behind them as they walk down the aisle. The reality of adding a long train is that you end up with so much extra fabric that will need to be bustled up before you go in to cocktails. Not only is this heavy to carry, but it can look huge. This is why we often suggest brides have a long veil instead. It looks just as beautiful but is far more practical.

Now, let's talk about the size of the skirt. While large skirts can look lovely and bring that fairy-tale energy to a bridal look, in reality, they can make moving around difficult. These skirts were fine when brides (and women in general) were less mobile, but in this day and age of getting in and out of cars and walking through fields to get the perfect photo, they can really complicate things. Again, this is a perfect example of something looking fabulous on the pedestal in the store but lacking functionality in the real world. That said, there are plenty of brides who still wear a full skirt, and my job is to explain the limitations so that there are no surprises.

Finally, consider upper-body mobility! So many brides focus on the bottom half of the dress and forget that they will need to move their arms and shoulders throughout the day. So, while you might love the off-the-shoulder trend that is taking over social media at the moment, you might reconsider if you want to hug family members and really express yourself on the dance floor later in the evening. There are ways to make off-the-shoulder sleeves detachable or a little bigger, but generally, your range of motion will be limited.

DON'T TRY TO REDESIGN A DRESS; IT DOESN'T WORK.

Like everything else with wedding dresses, knowing what you can and can't change about them is complicated. So I want to address the inevitable moment in dress shopping when you have found a dress that you think *could* be "the one" if you just changed a few things. My advice is to know yourself and proceed with caution.

A Dress with No "Buts"

Unless we are working with a client that ultimately wants a custom dress or has a strong ability to envision how something will look when modified, our goal is to find a dress that they love *as is*. This way they know exactly what they are getting and there shouldn't be any surprises. In fact, I like to tell my clients that an ideal situation is to find "a dress with no buts," meaning that if you find yourself saying, "I like it, *but* only if we can make the skirt/neckline/sleeves/embroidery like this," it's probably not your dress. This is where your ability to visualize is *really* important. If you can see in your mind what it will look like, and you know you'll like it, then you should be fine. But if you aren't sure or can't quite see it, then I would keep shopping.

To me, the ability to visualize something is different for everyone and yet another thing that has a spectrum, and each person falls at a different point. It's very important to understand your threshold for it when wedding dress shopping so you will know how comfortable you are making possible changes to the dress. I've put together a quiz on our website of questions that I ask our clients to understand their abilities. I encourage you to take this quiz and use the knowledge to inform your decisions.

If you are open to making changes to a dress and know that you can trust the process, it's important to have a basic understanding of what should be done in the production of the dress (and specified when ordering it) and what should be done in alterations after the dress comes in. This will help you to understand what is and *isn't* possible when considering changes to a dress. It will also help you to identify your motivations. Wanting to tweak a dress by reducing the sleeves or making it into a V-neck is a lot different from wanting to swap out a skirt, change a waistline, or remove an underwire. If you find yourself wanting too many changes, take it as a sign to find a different dress.

To give you a better idea of what changes should be made during the production of the dress and what can be done in fittings, I have a list that you can access on the website.

What if a consultant *swears* something not on the list can be done? Before making the purchase, ask to speak to the person doing the fittings to make sure it will look like what you want

it to. Every designer is different in terms of the alterations they will make—and allow to be made—to one of their dresses. However, my advice is to stick with two modifications *at maximum*. More than that and you should probably choose a different dress.

At this point you may be wondering about a fully custom wedding dress. I have lots to say about this, and you can access more information with the QR code at the end of the chapter.

UNDERSTAND THE ORDER DEADLINE

As you know by now, made-to-order wedding dresses can take a long time to make, and the orders need to be placed well in advance. But what the actual order deadline is varies greatly by designer. Some can do a shorter timeline with a rush fee, others can't rush dresses at all, and for others it's dependent on the particular dress and whether or not they have the fabric/lace/embroidery in stock or can get them in time. All of these factors contribute to the order deadline that can't be changed.

However, every once in a while you will encounter a consultant who scares the bride into thinking she has to make a quick decision—a way to encourage the bride to purchase. This tactic

is not OK, and I won't work with consultants who do this. For example, if the consultant says something like, "You really need to decide by X date because dresses are taking a really long time to make." Instead of feeling pressure and rushing into a decision, asking the following questions will provide more clarity:

1. If I can't make that deadline and I want to order later, is that possible with a rush fee?
2. Does the rush fee change depending on when the dress is ordered?
3. At what point can I no longer order the dress?

You'll send a clear message that you need more time and get the valuable information you need to make your decision. If you are feeling rushed and unable to make a decision by the deadline, to me that's a sign that there is too much doubt and it's not the right dress. Trust your instincts.

Scan this QR code for additional resources from this chapter.

Chapter 8

THE DECISION

AT THIS POINT, you have tried on many dresses and have probably fallen in love with a few dresses that look great, make you feel beautiful, and fit into your budget. So, how do you know when you've found THE one and you can stop looking at others? This is a question I get asked almost daily, mainly because so many brides are worried about making the wrong choice. The good news is that I have a method I call the Shine Test that works for every bride, regardless of your budget, decision-making style, or how many opinions you have swirling around you.

It's totally normal to love more than one dress, and it's funny how often I hear my clients tell me that they were worried they wouldn't find anything they liked, and now they have too many to choose from! It's a good problem to have, but it can also be difficult to navigate, especially if you are a Maximizer like me. So I'm going to teach you some of the techniques I use with my clients to help them.

RECENCY BIAS

This economic term, popular among the business school set, is surprisingly relevant to your wedding dress search. The concept essentially suggests that your preferences can be influenced by the recency of your experiences. In layman's terms, you're likely to remember and prefer the dresses you tried on toward the end of the day more vividly than those at the beginning. While photos can be really helpful, I strongly recommend scheduling follow-up appointments to try on your top contenders once more before making a final decision. If possible, arrange these appointments in the morning (back-to-back) when you're feeling fresh and have the most energy. This will give you the truest sense of how you feel wearing each one.

One final word of caution: I don't recommend that you send pictures to your family and friends before doing the following exercise. You need to know how you feel before you ask someone's opinion because you can easily get an answer you don't like. Decide for yourself, because you are the one wearing it and your opinion is the only one that matters.

The Shine Test

1. **Visualization:** Can you see yourself walking down the aisle in this dress? Imagine your aisle, however it will be—short or long, inside or outdoors. Put yourself in the moment that the doors close behind your maid of honor and reopen to find everyone looking at you for the first time. Are you in this dress? Do you think it goes with the setting and vibe of your wedding? If yes, then it stays in the running.
2. **Function:** Next, let's put it through the functionality test. How you feel in your dress is an important part of how you look on your wedding day.
    a. Temperature—Will you be hot or cold in this dress?
    b. Movement—Can you freely walk around in the dress and dance in it when it's bustled? (On that note, do you like how it looks bustled? Because it will be like that for your entire reception.)
    c. Weight—Is it heavy? If it feels heavy in the store, it's going to be magnified times ten on your wedding day.
3. **Comfort:** I know a lot of people will suggest that it's normal, and even honorable, to "suffer for fashion," but I am here to tell you that I could not disagree more. Looking beautiful is important, but *feeling* beautiful is the most important. That's going to be a lot harder if you aren't physically comfortable in your dress (or shoes or headpiece). Also, it's important to remember that any initial discomfort will amplify as the event progresses. An eight-hour day with a dress squeezing your ribs, chafing your arms, or limiting how you walk won't be fun.

Once you've considered these three elements, you will have analyzed the critical parts of a wedding dress, whether it's still in the running, and if it's a strong contender. Do this for each dress you are considering and compare your answers.

HOW TO ANALYZE

First, compare your favorite dresses side by side with a collage app. This comparison tool is incredibly helpful and will really allow you to analyze what you like and don't like about a dress. Remember in the last section when I told you to try and make the same pose at least once in each dress? This is why. It's so much easier to compare the dresses if you are generally standing the same way in each.

Next, apply the Shine Test. This is an easy three-point system I use with my clients to evaluate if a dress is *the one*.

These techniques will help you make a decision that feels right for you and have the confidence to make the purchase. Use the QR code at the end of the chapter to get your own worksheet. Once you fill this out, you are going to have a pretty clear view of which one is your favorite!

How do you react?

Having worked with so many brides over the years, I can tell you that women react in many different ways when it comes to finding their "perfect" dress. Some cry, some don't and feel like they should, and some brides know it's *the one* because they don't want to take it off. But then there's the group that just has a tough time deciding, no matter how much they love the dress, and for them time is the key. The point is, know yourself and think about how you make decisions in other areas. You may not be a crier, and that's OK. Just don't expect tears.

Other questions to ask yourself (if needed):

If the Shine Test hasn't eliminated all the dresses except one, then you need to ask yourself a few more questions:

- **Does the dress feel authentic to you?** So, what if you find a gorgeous dress that fits like a glove and looks spectacular but just doesn't feel like *you*? Keep looking. While you want to *wow* on your wedding day, choosing a design that doesn't align with your core signature style is risky, and not in a good way. It doesn't matter how stunning you look, if you don't *feel* like yourself, you're inevitably going to be self-conscious. This means that no matter how wonderful the night is and how gorgeous your photos are, you will always remember feeling awkward and uncomfortable when you look at your wedding album, and that will impact your memory of the day. Those who love you will also see that something is wrong.

  I once went shopping for a dress with a lovely mother and daughter and when we were comparing two dresses side-by-side, the mother said, "I can see she's much more comfortable in this dress." I looked at the photos and the daughter had what seemed like an identical smile in each of them but her mother "just knew," and she was right. The daughter bought that dress and loved it.

- **Are you OK with the required undergarments (if needed)?** A lot of brides don't think about their undergarments beyond buying something "special," but it's important to consider what will be needed under your dress on the actual day. Some brides are fine wearing Spanx on their wedding day while others would view it as a form of torture. There's no right or wrong answer here; it's really about what you're comfortable with.
- **Are you coordinating with your partner?** Thinking about what your fiancé will be wearing is an important piece because you want the level of formality to be the same. You don't want to be in a super formal beaded gown if your fiance is wearing a jacket and tie.

  It's a little more complicated with two brides because the options for what you can wear are endless. It could be that you both wear dresses, one woman wears a suit, both women wear suits/pants, one woman wears a different color . . . you get the idea. I come back to the principle that the formality level should be the same. You don't want one person to be black-tie ready and another to be casual chic.

  Here are a few things to think about if you are two brides trying to make a decision:

  - **If you are both wearing white, do the shades of white blend well together?** As you will learn pretty quickly in this process, there are *a lot* of variations of white/ivory, so just make sure one won't stand out as being much brighter in photos.
  - **If you choose different colors, how do they coordinate?** Do they look too similar? If you are both wearing dresses, are they each distinct enough that they don't look the same from afar?
- **Are there any "buts"?** Really think about it and if there is anything that you wish you could change about the dress. Do you have any hesitations about an element of it? If you do and it can't be modified, then it's not the one.
- **Do you have any doubts?** Doubt means *don't.* This is one of my favorite quotes from Oprah Winfrey. I have seen this maxim in action time and time again in bridal salons all over the world. While it doesn't always ring true in daily life, when it comes to wedding dress shopping, too many reservations is a pretty clear sign it's not the right dress.

Finally—and this is really important—never, *ever* buy a dress for the body you hope to have. You are beautiful **as you are now**. Not only is this not healthy, but you can also end up wasting money and not having a dress for your wedding day if you don't reach your goal or the weight loss doesn't leave your body shape in the way you expected it to. It's also much easier to make a larger dress smaller than it is to create room in a dress that is a size (or more) too small, so just don't do it.

SHOULD YOU WEAR A SECOND "DANCING" DRESS?

For some brides, this is a very cut-and-dried decision. Many have always wanted to wear a second dress because they love the drama and fun it adds to the evening. For others, it's a hard no; they want to wear their wedding dress for as long as they can since it's the only chance they will ever have to wear it. Then, there are brides in the middle who wonder whether a second dress is right for them. As with so many elements of a wedding wardrobe, there really is no right or wrong answer here; it all comes down to how *you* feel. Personally, I am a big fan of changing into a second dress because it allows you to dance, relax, and let loose in a way that's fun and *comfortable.*

Expense of a Second Dress

While it may sound like a luxury, a second dress doesn't have to be expensive. Lucky for us there are tons of adorable party dresses at great price points on the market, particularly during the holidays. So this question is less about budget and more about whether or not you want to change.

Let me explain: When most brides think of how long they will be in their dress, they usually think about the time between the beginning of the wedding and the end of the reception, but that's actually not the case at all. In fact, most brides are in their dress at least two hours before they arrive at the ceremony and even longer if they are doing first-look photos. This means there is a good chance you will be in your dress for six to eight hours or more. It's important to remember that wedding dresses are made differently; even the lightest wedding dress will feel different from your ready-to-wear clothing. This could be the way it's constructed or because you are wearing a corset or Spanx and feel like you can't breathe easily.

No matter how much you love your dress, you are going to be excited to take it off. I realize that this may sound a little surprising (especially to your mom, who lived in a generation when this was decidedly not a thing). But it's my job to prepare you, and I can tell you this for sure: When you slip into your second dress, you will immediately relax and let loose. You are going to be so much more comfortable and it's going to allow you to *party*. So take it from me, someone who has worked with many, many brides: you are going to love your dress, but you will hit a point where you are ready to take it off.

Also, as a person who loves a plan B (and C, D, and E), it is a really good idea to have something to change into in case something happens to your wedding dress. For example, I recently worked with a bride who, despite my advice otherwise, didn't buy a second dress, and because she wasn't able to travel back to New York, I wasn't there with her for her fittings that she did in her hometown. Long story short, on the wedding day her bustle broke and we had to fix it twice for her. But because the train was really long and there was a lot of fabric to deal with, we were unsure if our on-site fixing was going to stay. One of my dressers did an amazing job and sewed it up, and luckily it stayed all night. But before we left the wedding, she said that she wished she had listened to my advice and gotten a second dress so she would have had a backup plan if the bustle came out again.

I met another bride who told me her story of how someone spilled an entire glass of red wine on her at the reception and she ended up taking the dress off and soaking the spot in the bathtub and using a hairdryer to dry it. (I do not recommend that course of action at all, by the way.)

And I know of yet another bride who had a very expensive, gorgeous custom-made wedding dress, and when she sat down to dinner at her reception, the zipper split and she had to change into her dancing dress much earlier than she wanted to.

I could go on and on with stories like this, but my point is that it's always good to have a second dress even if it's not expensive and you know up-front you may never wear it. Better to be safe than sorry.

Here are the six main reasons to consider a second dress:

1. It's a fashion moment. There is nothing more fun than making your second entrance in a second dress. Everyone will go crazy for it!
2. Along those lines, it really amps up the party. It tells your guests, "I am ready to dance," and your guests will follow. This is something a lot of my brides talk about. It really does set the tone.
3. You can't dance when you feel constricted or are wearing something that's big or heavy.
4. Your wedding dress will most likely have a train that will be bustled. There is a good chance that it will come undone at some point despite your best efforts, and that makes it hard to dance.
5. It's just so much more comfortable. I've had brides buy *really* expensive dresses and change out of them way before the designated time because they were itchy, scratchy, or uncomfortable to wear.
6. As stated above, it's always good to have a backup plan if something happens to your dress.

If you decide to wear a second dress, it's important that it still goes with the overall feeling of your wedding. While you can definitely go with something outrageous—and I encourage you to do so if it feels good to you—you have to keep in mind the context of your event. If you are having a black-tie wedding, I think your second dress should stay in that feeling.

Lately, I've been advising my clients who have a formal wedding to change into a long dress rather than short because all of their female guests will be in long dresses. You have a lot of creative freedom at this moment, so have fun with it!

Think twice before doing a third dress.

At this point, some brides love the idea of an outfit change so much that they want to do it again! However, I typically advise against doing a third change, unless under very special circumstances. And the reason is this: It takes too much time. On your wedding day, and in life, time is the ultimate currency. Your wedding day will go by so quickly that most couples look back and remember it as a blur.

If you are considering it, do a cost-benefit analysis to make sure it's worth taking valuable time out of your day, time that you can't get back, to change again. With lots of experience, I can tell you that we estimate that each outfit change takes twenty minutes, sometimes longer. Think about it: You have to leave the party and get to the changing location, take care of the necessities, freshen up, possibly have a hair and makeup touch-up, change your outfit, shoes, and jewelry, and get back to your party. Is the third outfit worth it? Only you can decide what is right for you. Another option we suggest when one of our clients really wants three looks is to try and find something convertible rather than a full change (taking a piece off such as an overskirt or jacket) or even have a dress where you can take off part of the skirt and it becomes a mini dress. Whatever you decide, just make sure that it's worth the time away from your new spouse, guests, and party.

Scan this QR code for additional resources from this chapter.

Chapter 9

FITTINGS

IT DOESN'T MATTER HOW beautiful a dress is; if it doesn't fit well, it's not going to look good or be comfortable to wear. So if there is one thing every bride should know about buying a wedding dress, it's that a dress comes to life when it's fitted. Its true beauty is revealed when a seamstress pulls a little here, tucks in a little there, and makes it look like it was made for your body and yours alone.

With that said, it's definitely a process to get it right, and it takes time to do the work. Of course, each dress and woman are different, so the fitting process will depend on the bride, the dress, the fitter, and if and how the bride's body changes throughout the process.

Which leads me to a *really important* point. If you are someone who wants to lose weight or tone up before your wedding, you need to **be as close as you can to your goal for the first fitting**. I am by no means saying that you should change your appearance, but it's very common that brides want to do so, and I'm here to tell you that significant weight changes after fittings start are an alterations nightmare for everyone involved.

It's much better to be your fighting weight (or as close to it as you can be) before you step into the ring and your alterations process begins. Five pounds is not going to make a big difference on most frames, but any more than that and you're going to have to continue altering it so that it fits. That may not sound like a big deal, but you risk the integrity of the dress every time you open it up and take it in, so the more you do that at every fitting, the worse it's going to look.

I once had a bride that lost so much weight between the final fitting and the two weeks to her wedding that when I arrived onsite the dress was falling down her. It was an extremely expensive and intricate custom dress that had to be handled with care, and a sewing machine was necessary to do the work. We found a local seamstress to come and take it in as much as possible. While the embroidery on the seams didn't line up as it should have, the dress stayed up, which was the most important thing.

GUIDE TO FITTINGS

Here is a general guide to the life cycle of wedding dress fittings and what to expect.

Selecting a Fitter

The person doing your alterations is incredibly important, and it's essential that they have extensive experience with wedding dresses. Here is what you need to know about finding the best person for the job.

In-house fittings: Many bridal salons have in-house fittings, and whenever possible I highly encourage you to use them, even if it means having to travel. The reason I suggest this is two-fold:

- First, the in-house fitter is going to be the most familiar with the dress and is therefore the best person to fit it. It's common for them to have worked on the exact dress before and know a lot about the construction and the best way to alter it.
- Second, if, God forbid, something goes wrong in the fittings, the store has to fix it. If the alterations are done elsewhere, the store isn't responsible for the garment once it leaves their premises—and it is much harder to solve the issue. Even a commonplace request, like needing extra fabric or embroidery, has an added step when you are using an external fitter because (a) it won't be lying around the workroom and (b) you will have to be the one to contact the store, order the fabric, and make sure it gets to the fitter in enough time for the work to be done before the next fitting. Totally doable but just much easier if you don't have to get involved.

External fittings: When it's not possible to use an in-house fitter because they don't have one (sadly becoming more common for cost-saving purposes) or it's just not feasible for you to travel back to the place where you purchased the gown, you are going to need to find a reputable fitter in your area. As mentioned above, this person needs to be a bridal fitter and have extensive experience with wedding dress alterations. Here is how to find someone near you:

- Call your local bridal salon and ask if they have a fitter/alterations referral in your area.
- You can also ask a local wedding planner; chances are, they will have a good referral. For your reference, we've compiled a list that you can access by scanning the QR code.

When Fittings Start

You should expect your wedding dress fittings to begin about two months (give or take) before your wedding. This is the ideal timing because, if you plan on toning up and slimming down, you've had time to achieve most of your physical goals, and it gives the fitter enough time to do the work.

Number of Fittings

The average number of fittings you can expect to have is three. This can vary slightly on a case-by-case basis, but rarely are there only two. More often we add a fourth if there are tweaks to be done from the third fitting, and it is added as a try-on to make sure the dress is perfect.

You may be wondering why you must have three fittings when the dress was made-to-order for you. Well, remember when we spoke about how, most typically, your measurements are taken and applied to a size chart? This is when that size becomes shaped to your body.

But even with dresses that are made-to-measure (when designers take 30-plus measurements and create a dress form to mimic your body), you can expect to have three fittings.

What to Bring to Your Alterations/Fittings

- **Your wedding shoes:** Hemming a dress is a big job and having to re-hem it because you forgot your shoes is costly and time-consuming (and frustrating for the seamstress). If for some reason you haven't decided on an exact pair yet, you need to commit to a heel height and stick to it. Also, if you plan on changing into a different pair of shoes for the reception, bring those as well so you can check the hem for both.
- **Your veil or headpiece and all accessories:** This includes necklaces, earrings, and bracelets.
- **Undergarments:** If you know that you will most likely need undergarments, you will want to bring lots of different options (plain nude or white with minimum embellishments and lace), and different versions of the same product (a long-line corset, for example). The reason for this is that each piece will look different under the dress. Some might bulge, others might show through—you want to be sure you catch any issues up-front.
- **Shapewear:** If you plan to wear something to smooth and sculpt, bring multiple options with different levels of control that hit at different places.
- **Camera:** It's great to have photos from the appointment, but more importantly, you are going to want to video the bustle being done so the person doing it on the wedding day has a reference.

WHAT HAPPENS AT EACH FITTING

Your fitter may work in a slightly different order, but I've been in thousands of wedding dress fittings, and this is a pretty good rundown of how it typically goes.

The First Fitting

Your first wedding dress fitting is a big deal, and it's really common for brides to be "exservous" (a word my kids made up that's a combination of *excited* and *nervous*—and so appropriate here). Brides are often really excited to see their dress and put it on for the first time but are also worried about how any changes done in production turned out, how it fits, and if they will still love it. Knowing what to expect from this first fitting will help you to be mentally prepared and give you a leg up in the process.

First and foremost, remember that the work has yet to be done, so it will not initially be as flattering as it will be once alterations are complete. Fittings are a process that evolves over a two-month period, so don't worry if you put it on and don't feel 100 percent amazing. I see it all the time, and with tweaks and changes made in the alterations it will gradually come to life as you envisioned it. This can be a little scary, I know, but trust the process.

At this fitting, the bulk of the pinning is going to be done, and this is often the longest fitting. (I typically allot an hour and a half.)

Steps of the First Fitting

1. I like to start by getting the bride's overall temperature for how she's feeling and have a discussion with the fitter on what generally needs to be done. If you are planning on making design changes to the dress that were advised to happen in fittings (and not production), this is a great time to discuss them. It's so simple, really, but this conversation can alleviate a lot of tension for the bride because she knows that her concerns (if she has any) will be addressed.
2. Next the fitter will start assessing the different areas of the dress and pin accordingly. They will start at the top and work their way down, because what happens on the bodice will affect how the skirt falls and the length.
3. Once the bodice has been fitted, the work on the skirt can begin. Remember: You *must* have your shoes for the first fitting. The skirt length is a critical piece of this fitting and important to work on between the first and second so it can be perfected over the three.
4. If you have ordered a veil through the store and you would like to try it on with your dress, now is the time to do it. You want to be able to see it with the train down and not pinned up into the bustle (more on that below) so you can get the total effect and check the length.
5. Last comes pinning the bustle. At this point your fitter is going to show you options for how to bustle if you have any with your dress. If you don't like what you see, ask her for other options. Most fitters have a preferred way of bustling, and it's OK to challenge them on alternatives, but also listen to them if they tell you it won't work because, at the end of the day, they are the expert.

6. The bulk of the alterations on your dress happen between the first and second fittings, so this is the longest spacing between the appointments. Typically, your second fitting will be scheduled for at least a month later so they have time to do the work.

The Second Fitting

The second fitting is much easier (and generally shorter) than the first because you will really start to see the alterations shape it into what you want it to be. You are going to put your dress on and see it start to come to life. My clients often say they are able to breathe a sigh of relief at this fitting because it becomes real.

The major things happening at this fitting are:

- The alterations that have been made are checked and further tweaked if needed.
- The dress is assessed to see whether it needs to be taken in more.
- The hem, now that it's been basted (when the fabric is sewn but not cut so there is room to make changes), is checked when walking.
- The train is typically not bustled at the start of the fitting, and the fitter will do it while you are there. At this point you can assess how it looks and make sure that it is not dragging.

Bustles

On a very basic level, bustling a wedding dress simply means pulling up the train in the back and securing it so that it's floor-length and you're able to walk around and dance and greet your guests without stepping on your dress. There are three main types of bustles, and every seamstress has his or her own way of executing them.

The American Bustle

This is when you take the fabric from the outside of the dress and lift it up to a higher point on the dress. Depending on the amount of fabric and design, you may need several different points.

The French Bustle

This is where the fabric is gathered underneath the dress, creating a "bubble" effect.

The Hemline Bustle

This is where the train of the dress is turned inside of the hem, just off of the floor. We see this one the least in our business simply because most dresses have too much fabric for this to work.

Now, to complicate matters even more, there are **combinations of the three** that fitters will do when a dress has multiple layers, so you can easily end up with a dress that has a bustle that is one-part French, one-part American, and sometimes, even a hemline bustle will be thrown in there.

American French Hemline

- The way to make sure your bustle stays in place is to ensure that **no part of your dress touches the floor at any time.** If it is, I promise you it will be stepped on. This point of view is a bit controversial because, like many people, I agree a dress looks prettier when it is sweeping the floor (and this is why so many fitters will suggest leaving it a little longer), but trust me when I tell you, it's not worth it. If you want to avoid a lot of hassle, I suggest that you keep it a full inch off the ground in the back.
- The second fitting is a great time to try out your accessories. If you are unsure of what jewelry, hair accessories, or coverage options you are going to wear, now is the time to try them on and make your decision.
- Typically, the veil is not tried on at this fitting unless it was altered. Because it's delicate, it's better not to handle it too much.
- Normally there is less to be done from the second to third fitting, and there are about two weeks between them.

What Does Basting Mean?

I want to familiarize you with this term because you are going to hear it a lot at your first fitting. *Basting* is when the alteration is made and sewn, but the fabric is not cut. Fitters do this so that the alterations can be assessed and corrected if needed.

The Third Fitting

You've made it, and you are almost done! The third and typically final fitting is when you really see the dress as it will be and feel.

Your dress should be just a little bit snug, as wedding dresses work somewhat like jeans in that they stretch out a bit once on the body. It's also common for brides to lose an extra pound or two the final week before the wedding even if they aren't trying, so you run the risk of it being a little big on the wedding day. If it's not there already, it's a good idea to have your fitter add a grosgrain belt around the waist, which will give you the option for a tighter setting if you need it. Otherwise, I suggest that you make the dress fitted to you (particularly at the waist) and be comfortably snug. You should, of course, be able to move and breathe!

Here's what to expect at the final fitting:

- The fit is checked again and any necessary tweaks made.
- The length is reviewed one more time by walking around.
- Have fitters show you how to do the bustle **and take a video of it being done.** Every fitter has a different system for creating the bustle, so you will want them to point out what to look

What Length Should Your Dress Be?

Brides often worry about the length of their dress and what is appropriate and looks best. The general rule of thumb is that it should be about a half-inch off the floor, and you want to make sure when you walk it isn't turning under at all. You also want to take into consideration the terrain you will be walking on. If you are going to be on grass or carpet, you will want to make the dress a little shorter because the ground height will affect the length. I always err on the side of shorter because the dress will grow throughout the night (just like jeans stretch out with wear) and can easily become a tripping hazard.

for. (Strings versus buttons and loops? Color-coded versus numbered? How many of each? Do you have to cut the chain holding the layers together?) This piece is critical because it can be confusing even to a seasoned pro without knowing what to look for.

- Discuss handling the dress with your fitter. Ask them what you should do if it's wrinkled. Can it be steamed or is it better to use a cool iron? Are there any other things you should be aware of?
- If you are picking it up, arrange for a time that you will do so, and if you are shipping, confirm the logistics (shipping date, overnight delivery, signature required—always the case with wedding dresses, so make sure there is someone to receive it).

A Fourth and Final Try-On

Sometimes, if there is work being done after the third fitting, we recommend going back and checking it one final time to avoid any surprises on the wedding day. This extra appointment isn't the norm, but if you are on the fence and it works logistically, it's always better to do it.

HOW TO TRAVEL WITH YOUR DRESS

It's estimated that one-quarter of brides choose to have destination weddings, and many others travel back to their (or their partner's) hometown for their big day. This means that there is a good chance you will need to travel with your dress. Knowing how to do that properly is essential—and it will eliminate a lot of potential stress.

First, let's talk about packing.

Ensuring that your dress has been packed properly is critical to the condition it arrives in, and the good news is that most bridal salons will steam and pack the dress for you. To prevent the bust from caving in, they will make a bodice out of cardboard and tissue

paper that will keep the shape. Don't be concerned if this adds more bulk to the form—this will keep it looking good. Next, they will cover the dress in a layer of plastic before putting it in a large garment bag. This extra layer not only protects it from getting wet, but it makes sure that it doesn't rub against the garment bag and get damaged. If you are traveling with your dress, and either of these things weren't done at the salon where you bought it, ask a top dry cleaner in your area to do it for you. A great resource for finding one is www.WeddingGownSpecialists.com.

Now that your gown is stuffed and packed, you have to figure out how to get it where you need it to go with the least amount of stress possible.

Here are the pros and cons of shipping versus carrying it with you.

Carrying It With You

Let's start by talking about taking it with you.

This is often the best choice for brides who are nervous about letting the gown out of their sight. As a worrier myself, I understand brides who choose to take this route. However, it's important to know this isn't the easiest choice in a lot of cases. Depending on the size of your dress, the garment bag can range from small to big to huge, making it cumbersome and difficult to deal with. If you are fortunate enough to be driving it somewhere, it's definitely a lot easier; you will just want to make sure you lay it as flat as possible in your car.

Things become significantly more complicated if you are flying because there are several things you have to consider. Maneuvering through the airport with a huge garment bag isn't easy. Not to mention, having to do things like putting it through the security machine and folding it over your arm can wrinkle the dress.

What Is a Wrap-around Fitting?

For brides traveling from out of town, the back-and-forth to a different city can be difficult before the wedding. In those cases we often schedule what we call a wrap-around fitting for the second and third ones. The first fitting always happens on its own because there is so much work to be done, but after that, we will have our brides come to New York for two or three days and get the next two fittings in during that time. Some salons will charge a fee for this service, but it's almost always less than the cost of an additional trip.

Bringing It on the Plane

You can call ahead and tell the airline that you are bringing a wedding dress, which is worth a shot, but honestly, I don't know how much good it does. The unfortunate reality is that you can't always trust that information is going to make its way to the crew. As you embark, you can ask the stewardess to hang it in the closet on the plane, and most are happy to do this. But again, this isn't foolproof. Larger gowns require more space, which isn't usually available in these closets that almost certainly have other items in them. One time on my way to a client's wedding in Istanbul, I was told that it wouldn't fit and to find another solution. In this case, I was able to fold it up and put it in an overhead bin because the dress was slim and fully beaded, so I knew that wouldn't damage it. But of course, that's not the case with all—*or even most*—dresses.

If carrying it on the plane with you really feels like the right option, and the garment bag that it's in will be large (because you have a fuller skirt), the safest (but by no means the cheapest!) option is to purchase an extra seat for the dress. I've actually done this before and it was hilarious, because the dress had a meal selection in first class. Nothing better than two desserts! One other quick tip on this is to be sure to place it safely between you and the window to protect it from spills.

	Pros	Cons
Driving with Your Dress	You can control how it is handled and when it arrives.	May require a large vehicle because the dress needs to lie flat with nothing on top of it.
Flying with Your Dress—Carrying It	Never leaves your possession.	Can be difficult to carry through the airport and store on the plane.
Flying with Your Dress—Checking It	Easier to navigate the airport and less wear and tear on the dress.	Possibility that your bag can get lost. Always use an AirTag if you opt for this choice.
Shipping Your Dress Domestically	The dress is carefully stuffed and packed and therefore arrives in good condition.	Delivery requires a signature, so someone needs to be at the destination to sign. Possibility of delays.
Shipping Your Dress Internationally	Recommend only if you have several large garments to send or you aren't going straight to your venue.	Expensive and often complicated by customs. Possibility of delays.

If all of this just seems like too much, another option is checking it. Yes, you heard me right; you can fold that baby up and put it in a suitcase! That is, of course, if you can tolerate the risk of not having it by your side. If you are flying first class, the chances that your luggage may be displaced, lost, or delayed go down a lot because they mark each bag as "priority." Still, I suggest putting an Apple AirTag in the suitcase. The advantage of checking it is that it makes it much easier to get through the airport, and there is less handling of the dress. But being a person who tries to avoid risk at all costs, I can't imagine not worrying about it on the entire flight. At least with the AirTag you will know it's on the plane.

Checking the dress works best if your dress is tulle or lace because they don't wrinkle or crease easily, especially if it is a slimmer silhouette. If it's a thicker fabric like faille or mikado, it can also work but probably only if it's a slim gown. If it's a ball gown and a stiffer fabric, you may be hard-pressed to find a suitcase that will fit it. There are trunks you can purchase that are specifically designed to transport dresses, but they tend to be expensive. In fact, this is where the phrase "trunk show" comes from—they literally pack the dresses into trunks and ship them places.

Finally, if none of this sounds appealing, you can ship it.

Shipping the Dress

Your dress will be prepared the same way that we talked about before, and then placed into a large box suitable for shipping. The stores generally ship them overnight via FedEx or UPS and require a signature, so you have to make sure someone is home to receive it. Sometimes, you have to get creative because of this. One time, a wedding planner I was working with was tasked with receiving the client's dress but wouldn't be home during the UPS window and paid her neighbor's son to sit on her lawn and wait for the dress to arrive. One other quick note is to make sure that you avoid Friday shipments or Monday deliveries, because you don't want it sitting in a delivery truck over the weekend.

I will also say that you want to make sure you are not shipping the week of the wedding. I had a client recently who, for a series of unavoidable circumstances, had to have the dress shipped the Monday before the wedding. It was sent overnight, but FedEx decided it wasn't going to deliver it until Thursday, and her mother, who was receiving it, was leaving for the wedding on Wednesday. This was a *very* stressful situation, to say the least, and thankfully FedEx found the box and got it to the local office where the family could pick it up. I wouldn't wish that kind of stress on my worst enemy, so take my word for it: ship early.

International Shipping

Now, let's say you're having an international wedding. I don't recommend shipping because there is a very good chance it can get stuck in customs, and that is something you definitely don't want to deal with. The only way shipping makes any sense is to hire a specialty company to do it for you. There are companies that will pick the dress up at your home and ensure that it arrives at its destination on time. It's not inexpensive, but it's *much* better than dealing with customs and delays.

I know that this has been a lot of information and there are so many nuances with weddings in general that it feels like a never-ending list of if-then statements. But you are doing great, and you've made it so far! Now you are ready to accessorize!

Scan this QR code for additional resources from this chapter.

Chapter 10

ACCESSORIES AND BEAUTY

THE HARDEST PART IS finished and you have found and purchased a dress that you love, and it's time to add the finishing touches that will make it all come together. From veils and earrings to hairpieces, jewelry, and bags, we are about to discuss the many ways you can elevate and enhance your look with the use of accessories.

Before I go any further, I need to put this out there as bluntly as I can: I absolutely adore accessorizing and firmly believe that the right pieces can bring a look to life, but please, **don't gild the lily**. More isn't always better; in fact, it is often much worse. Having worked in this industry for as long as I have, I can safely say that knowing when to layer—and when to lay off—is not only useful when dressing oneself, it's often the difference between looking polished and looking like you are trying too hard. I always advise my clients to think of the great Coco Chanel, who suggested that we all "get fully dressed and then take one thing off." I have found that this works well in most scenarios, but it's especially helpful when putting together your wedding ensemble.

Here's another secret to looking great: Choose pieces you *really* love and that are special to you (or will become special because you wore them on your wedding day). Don't allow anyone to pressure you to wear things that don't feel right (i.e., your future mother-in-law's antique earrings that have been in the family for generations). I know that it can be hard to know where to start. But if we take it step-by-step, we will get there.

A FEW THINGS TO CONSIDER BEFORE WE BEGIN

1. Will any of your accessories be your "something borrowed"?
2. Are there any family heirloom pieces you want to incorporate? Often my clients have a piece of jewelry from a grandparent or other important person that they want to incorporate in some way, but this doesn't always mean they have to wear it. Sometimes we pin it to the dress or attach it to the bouquet. Don't be afraid to get creative!
3. What are you comfortable wearing day-to-day? Chances are, those preferences are for a reason, so don't deviate from that too much. For example, I hate heavy necklaces. When I wear one, I can't wait to take it off and do so immediately, sometimes before I even get home. So, for me, it would be very important not to do that on my wedding day. I've also had many clients who hate dangly earrings or bracelets that clink around when they wear them. Whatever your preferences are, stay true to them on your wedding day.
4. Bring many options to your second fitting to try them with your dress. If at all possible, I also recommend that you do your hair and makeup trial before the fitting as well. This will help you to get a good sense of what you will look like when it all comes together.

JEWELRY

Earrings

Of all of the jewelry worn on wedding days, earrings are the most common. Every single one of my brides has worn them and with good reason: The right pair can make cheekbones pop, add a bit of sparkle to your eyes, and frame your face with glittering light. This is why you will rarely see an actress at a premiere or big event without them. In fact, when asked about her "red carpet must-have," film icon Sophia Loren said, "A great pair of earrings, they add light and life to the face!"

That said, not all styles are created equal when it comes to the way they complement different face shapes. If you have a round face, for example, studs will make it rounder, whereas a beautiful tassel will give you length. For a square shape, try longer ovals to soften the jaw line, or geometric angles to emphasize it. Oval face shapes can wear anything, though stay away from anything too long, as that tends to lengthen the look. **For more face shapes, see the QR code at the end of the chapter.**

Monique

Necklaces

While they can be absolutely beautiful, necklaces are tricky because they can very easily make your wedding dress look like you're channeling Patti LuPone in *Evita*. (If you don't immediately know what I am talking about, head over to Google ASAP.) It's the reason 75 percent of my clients avoid them, and the other 25 percent choose something simple (such as a pendant or a diamond tennis necklace). If you do opt to wear one, make sure it flows with the neckline of your dress and keep your earrings small; this will keep everything in balance.

Bracelets

The first thing to consider when deciding if you should wear a bracelet is practicality. In other words, will it snag your dress? Sometimes when there are prongs holding stones, like with a diamond tennis bracelet, for example, it can snag or get caught on the material of your dress. This is most common with tulle, lace, or chiffon. The best way to know for sure is to do a test against a similar fabric (not your dress!) before wearing it. If you are in the clear and you love bracelets—go for it! If you're like most brides and don't know which wrist to wear it on, we always suggest the right, since your engagement ring and wedding band will be on the left.

Hair Accessories

While some hair accessories can be beautiful (many UK brides, for example, wear delicate headbands on their wedding day in place of veils), they can easily become overpowering. Remember what I said about gilding the lily? The key factors to consider are your hairstyle, what other jewelry you're wearing, and how it will look with your veil if you are wearing one. If you feel like your 'do needs some jazzing up, there are many different options to choose from: headbands, decorative hair pins and bobby pins, combs, halos, and barrettes. You can also use fresh flowers (and I recommend having backups in case they wilt throughout the night). The options are endless, so try a few different options at your hair trial and take pictures.

What about a tiara?

Did you notice the absence of tiaras above? My feeling is that unless you are aristocracy and it's a family heirloom, wearing a tiara can look costumey and steal the attention from your overall look. And yes, I did it in 2001 so I'm not throwing stones, but today I would advise myself against it.

TO VEIL OR NOT TO VEIL

Now let's talk about the veil. This is arguably the most traditional wedding accessory of all, and I find brides have strong opinions on it one way or the other. Some don't feel like a bride without one, whereas others feel like it's just not them. A few just aren't into the symbolism. Like everything else, it all comes down to your individual style.

Personally, I love them. I feel they add a real sense of drama and romance to your look, and let's be honest; your wedding day is the only time in your life that you can do it! If you want to wear one or at least give it a try, there are a lot of things to consider when it comes to choosing the best veil for you and your dress, so here are a few pointers:

- Whenever possible, purchase the veil at the same store where you buy your dress, and try to get one from the same designer if you can. It's the best way to make sure the color and length are a perfect match.
- Speaking of length, a veil should be at least 12 inches past the end of your dress train. I personally love a longer veil and use 24 inches as the minimum. Sometimes we go even longer from there!
- A veil is a terrific solution for brides who want a really long train on their dress but don't want to have the hassle of bustling all that fabric or simply don't have an option with their dress design.
- There are going to be people who disagree with me here, but I think a veil should always be long. Short veils are as short in length as they are on impact, and unless your dress is short also, my advice is to skip it.
- You don't need to have embellishments on a veil for it to be beautiful. In fact, if your dress has a lot of detail or lace, you may not even see the embellishments, and you are paying a lot more for very little gain.
- However, I absolutely love an embroidered style that extends the drama of the gown or one that is lace trimmed and frames the face. There are so many creative and beautiful options, so if it's in the budget (because they aren't cheap!), go for it!
- In the last few years, we've seen the rise of the colorful embroidered veil, and they are a fantastic way of adding a pop of color if you don't want it on your dress. I love pairing them with a simplistic dress for an added wow factor.

How long should my veil be?

When trying to decide which length is right for you, always take into account what your aisle is made of. If you are going to be inside and the path to the altar is smooth, you should be fine with

VEILS

any length you want. But if you are outside and on grass, stone, or some other material that can potentially catch the veil and snag it, you will want to keep it a little on the smaller side.

There are many different styles of veils to consider, all of which are illustrated on the opposite page, but I suggest choosing from the two long styles. Remember: Go long or go home!

Chapel-Length Veil: 90 Inches

A chapel-length veil is appropriate when you have a chapel-length train (12 inches to 18 inches from where it hits the floor) and you don't want something overly dramatic. It should always extend at least 12 inches past where the train ends and can go longer if you would like. I prefer having the veil 24 inches past the end of the train so it doesn't look skimpy.

The Blusher

Created to cover the bride's face, the blusher was used for a few different reasons in various cultures. Some brides believed it would protect them from evil spirits, while others used it to signify their purity. In arranged marriages, the blusher was used to hide the bride's face until the marriage was official, when the groom would lift it and see his wife for the very first time. I am so glad to be living today instead of back then!

Cathedral-Length Veil: 108–120 Inches

I adore cathedral-length veils and love using them to ramp up the drama while not adding more fabric to the dress. As a general rule, I'd keep it to no more than 36 inches past your train, or it starts to look a little funny and can become quite unruly to handle, especially outside. Quick tip: These veils don't have to be used only with cathedral-length trains (22 inches past where it hits the floor). They can be paired with shorter versions as well to up the grandeur of your look.

Veil Positioning

Many brides wonder where the veil comb should be placed on their head, and this is an important consideration when deciding on what hairstyle and accessories you will wear. While there is no strict rule about placement, I typically suggest brides place the veil on the top of their heads (rather than low by their necks) because it frames the face more beautifully. If you are unsure as to where that is, you can use the highest point of your ear as a guide and go directly up from there.

Blusher

A blusher is a piece of tulle that can be worn over the bride's face when she's walking down the aisle. Some blushers are part of the veil, and some are added pieces. If your veil does have one but you don't choose to wear it over your face, that's OK. It can stay behind and just be an added element that looks pretty. There is no right or wrong answer; it's just personal preference.

One word of caution: If you do plan on wearing it over your face, make sure the veil you purchase does not have an embroidered edge that goes all the way around. This is because when you wear the blusher, the embroidery will create a line in front and look strange in photos.

ACCESSORIES

Belts & Sashes

There was a period in the late 2000s when I rarely had a client who didn't wear a wide sash, sometimes one that was embellished with crystals or flowers or done in color. While that trend has certainly gone away and I'm not eager to see it return, I will say there are some advantages to wearing something at your waist. Not only does it draw it in, but it will hide the dress seam if there is one and can generally just finish off the look. It's not necessary to cover the seam, but some brides prefer it. True belts can also be a chic and modern way to accessorize your wedding dress.

At the end of the day, it's up to you, but here are some general guidelines to consider:

- **Keep it tonal:** The one thing you don't want people to do when you walk down the aisle is to look at the belt before looking at your face.
- **Change it up:** Once you have bustled your dress and taken off your veil, you can change into something more interesting. Sometimes, I will add a metallic belt to a simple crêpe gown, which really amps it up several notches and will give the look a great modern flair.
- **Keep it proportionate:** It's important that the belt work with your body type and the volume of the dress. You don't want it to look so small that it can't hold up the skirt or so wide that it takes up most of your torso.

Garter Belts

Today, most of the garter belts I come across are heirloom pieces that brides wear as their "something old." Most brides forgo the traditional garter toss at the reception. If you're considering wearing a garter, one thing to keep in mind is that today we have slimmer cut gowns, so you can often see the garter outline through the fabric if you are wearing one.

Handbags

For many brides, handbags and clutches are often an afterthought when it comes to planning their wedding ensemble, but this accessory not only serves an important function, it can work wonders when pulling your overall look together. While it's true they remain largely out of the spotlight, a great bag (read: functional, stylish, and easy to carry) can feel like a godsend when you need to slip off to the powder room to freshen up, and where else would you put your lipstick, tissues, mints, etc.? While some brides want their phones with them, others want to stay in the moment with the ones they love and have no need for it. That part is up to you, but if you want it in there, measure in advance to make sure it fits.

The key to finding one that fits your needs (and style) is to spend a bit of time on it. Here are things to consider:

- Will it close easily with all of your items in it?
- Does it coordinate with your dress?
- Do you want it to be your pop of color?
- Is it a piece that you want to keep as a memento?

That last one was important to me when I was shopping for a clutch, so much so that the lack of options was one of the things that prompted me to go to fashion school. Your wedding day is the time to buy pieces you will have forever, if that's important to you. Even after all these years, I still have and love mine and hope that my daughter will use it someday.

Shoes

Finally, let's talk about shoes! These are often the most popular accessory and where my brides tend to have the most fun. These days anything goes when it comes to what brides wear on their feet. I have seen everything from gold stilettos to Swarovski crystal-encrusted sneakers to hot pink velvet. It's an amazing way to express your personal style in a subtle way. The key to picking the right shoes is to make sure you're as comfortable wearing them as you are excited to look at them. This is not the time to spend big on a pair of sky-high Jimmy Choos when you have worn flats and kitten heels for the past five years!

Here are a few other things to consider when choosing your shoes.

- Where is your wedding taking place and when? What terrain you will be walking on is an important factor to the type of shoe you should choose.
- What are the textures and accents you love? Sparkle, lace, bling?
- How important is comfort to you personally? That was a trick question. If you say that it's not important on your wedding day, you're wrong. Discomfort is magnified on your wedding day. I cannot tell you the number of brides who have *sworn* to me that they will be comfortable in a super-high heel all night, just to end up in so much pain they take them off.
- Do you want classic white, or are you open to other colors? Will these be your "something blue"?

JIMMY CHOO

SHOES

- Do you want open-toed or closed? Strappy? I am a big fan of closed-toe with a slim wedding dress where the shoe will peek out when you walk. I think it gives a streamlined and clean look. If you have a fuller skirt, you won't see it when you walk, so it matters less.
- How high is too high?
- Do you want a heel at all?
- Will you have more than one pair?
- What is your budget?

For more information and help selecting the best shoe for you, refer to the guide we have on the website.

Gloves

As you may have noticed from my wedding picture, I'm a big fan of the bridal glove. I love the chic drama they add. While I don't have many brides asking me for them these days, they are still around and resurface at different moments. In particular, sheer gloves with embroidery have gained recent popularity and can be a beautiful and dramatic way of adding to your wedding-day look walking down the aisle.

Debunk the Myth That Your Shoes Won't Be Seen

People say to me all the time that "No one is really going to see the shoe," but this isn't entirely true; just look at my wedding picture in the introduction of the book. Here are the key moments when your shoes take center stage:

- The accessory photos that your photographer will take
- Going up or down stairs
- Sitting
- Kneeling during the service
- When you stomp the glass in a Jewish ceremony
- During your first dance, particularly if you are doing a dip

HAIR AND MAKEUP

You've picked your dress, love your shoes, and know exactly which earrings you plan to wear. Now it's time to think about hair and makeup.

While your sartorial choices get most of the fanfare when it comes to your wedding day, your hair and makeup are equally important. Like the accessories you choose to wear, how you appear from the neck up has a huge impact on your overall look and can enhance or distract from your dress. As I have said throughout this book: A bride can only look her best when she feels her best, and that can only happen when she feels like herself. So for your walk down the aisle, we recommend keeping it natural and classic and getting creative for your other events if you crave some drama.

With that said, hiring the right glam squad is one of the most important choices you make because they are in close proximity to you for a good part of your wedding day. When you know and trust those who are making you up, you can relax with the confidence that you will look like the most beautiful version of yourself and stay that way throughout the night—and that is worth the investment.

Now, before I go on, I want to be very clear that I am not a hair and makeup expert. But having spent twenty-plus years working alongside them, I've learned a few things about the dos and don'ts of hiring the best people for the job and creating a wedding day look that you love.

Get a clear vision of what you want.

A good starting point for inspiration is to go back to your Personal Style Cocktail that you determined in chapter 2. You can use those descriptors to guide so many elements of your style, including hair and makeup. If we use mine as an example (classic, feminine, with a touch of sparkle), it translates into natural makeup (classic), with my favorite red lipstick (feminine), and a pop of sparkle (sparkly eyeshadow). Classic and feminine hair (to me) is a beautiful chignon or bouncy curls. This information will be a great guide when it comes to assessing an artist's style and if they would be a good fit for you.

It's also a great idea to think about your everyday makeup when considering what you want to look like on your wedding day. For example, for better or worse, I never wear foundation. I just hate the feeling of it on my skin. Now, I understand that for event dressing, particularly with photos, it's important to smooth out the skin, so the test of a truly great makeup artist for me is that they can achieve that look without it feeling heavy and caked on. I can't tell you the number of times I've wiped it all off after the artist was finished. Making sure that didn't happen on my wedding day was a top priority for me, and I bet you know me well enough by now that it won't come as a surprise that I did trials with five makeup artists before finding the one who worked.

The same thing happened when finding a hairstylist, but I attribute that to life before Pinterest and not having a good example to show them. Plus, I have a lot of hair, and that's not always easy for people to deal with. At the end of the day, it worked out, and I was happy and comfortable in my look, but *wow*—was it a project getting there!

Another key piece is to consider what accessories you plan to wear and how important it is that they are *seen*. For example, if you love a great pair of heirloom earrings but want to wear your hair down, let your hairstylist know this beforehand so they can craft the look accordingly.

And finally, you know my favorite saying—don't gild the lily—and that goes for hair and makeup too. I love keeping it simple, clean, and classic for the ceremony, and then you can amp it up a bit more for the reception.

Ask for referrals, but don't rely on them.

Asking trusted friends and colleagues for their favorite hair and makeup artists is a great way to create a curated list, but it is important to remember that just because someone was great for your best friend doesn't mean they are right for you. This is especially true if your BFF has a different style or personality than you do.

Add all recommendations to your list and then do a deep dive. Look at their bridal portfolio, their Instagram gallery, their website, and any editorial work (photoshoots for magazines, newspapers, online outlets, etc.). Narrow it down to three and set up trials with them. Go in with a list of questions that will help you get a clear view of how they work, how well they listen, and who they like to work with and why.

Hire your team as early as you can.

This is not only to secure them for your wedding. The further out you can hire your team, the more time they have to guide you on things that will make you look even more beautiful on your wedding day. Makeup artists are great resources for skincare tips and teaching you how to practice wearing false eyelashes. Hairstylists can give you tips on how to ensure your hair looks its best by the time you walk down the aisle.

I had a bride start taking a hair-growth supplement seven months before her wedding (on the advice of her hairstylist and with her doctor's approval, of course), and the difference in her hair was astounding. It's also worth noting that if you plan to wear extensions or have extensions made for your wedding day, you will need a longer lead time. I recently did a wedding with a celebrity hairstylist who made a wig for the bride that they built different looks on all weekend.

Hire a team with wedding experience.

The thing with weddings is that they are different from other types of events. They have their own schedule, timing, and energy. Everything is heightened and it's important that whenever possible you work with people who have experience working them. However, if you fall in love with someone who doesn't typically do weddings or is just starting out, at least make sure they understand the strictness of timelines and the importance of things like snugly securing the veil.

I have seen even the most seasoned professionals derail the schedule by running behind. I've also experienced stylists fighting back about pinning the veil down because it might disrupt the hair, and guess what . . . one of these times the veil actually flew off the bride's head while she was going down the aisle on a windy day. It made for an adorable picture, but the point is that you should discuss these things beforehand and make a plan.

If you can get a team that has experience working together, do it.

Not only will this ensure things go smoother (and more efficiently), but the energy around you will be much calmer. Those who have a history of working together can usually move in and out

JONES ROAD

of each other's way with greater ease, and they will bring friendly and familiar energy, which will keep the mood light.

Do a trial for every look.

This includes, but is not limited to: your engagement party, your wedding day, your afterparty, and brunch if you are getting dressed (and not just rolling out of bed!). I love it when my clients really switch up their look for every fashion moment. Getting a little creative with the events before and after the wedding can be a fun and interesting way to show a whole different side of your personality. That's not for everyone, of course, so ultimately do what feels best and most comfortable to you.

Keep your team with you.

You may be inclined to let your hair and makeup team go once you are dressed because, after all, keeping them longer costs more. But you will need touch-ups throughout the day, especially when taking photos and before you go down the aisle. So if you can swing it financially, it's a really good idea to make sure your team is on hand to keep you looking pristine.

The ideal time to let your hair, makeup, and dressing team go is after the wedding dress is bustled and you are going in to cocktails. At that point, most brides don't need or want to do a lot of touch-ups and would rather spend their time enjoying the party. When our dressing team leaves, they have set up the second dress to change into with the accessories so it's all laid out and have also put the wedding dress garment bag there for safekeeping when it's taken off. Typically the hair and makeup teams have given them their lipstick, powder, and hairspray so that they are prepared if they need a little refresh throughout the night.

With all that said, if you're planning to change into a second dress for dancing or the after-party, some brides like to have their team stay for that. To me, the cost isn't always worth it, and it is only really necessary when you are doing a major change to your look. Either way, it's important to consider logistics. How long it will take, where you are doing it, and what it will entail (dress, hair, makeup, or all three). The goal is to do it as quickly and efficiently as possible so you can get back to the party.

Scan this QR code for additional resources from this chapter.

DUCHESS SATIN

Chapter 11

YOUR WEDDING FASHION STORY

AT THIS POINT, we've covered what you are going to wear from head to toe on your wedding day. This not only sets the tone for the other fashion choices for the wedding (of which there are many) but can also be used as inspiration for details incorporated into the wedding. Your wedding day look is really just the beginning of your bridal fashion journey, as the days are gone when a bride needed only to think about her wedding dress. Today there can be up to nine wedding weekend events, plus more that are held in advance. That translates into a lot of shopping, decisions, and preparation—big tasks even when not planning a wedding.

In this chapter, we are going to discuss how to create a beautiful, cohesive, and memorable fashion story that shows off your own unique style and coordinates effortlessly with the type of wedding you are having.

WHAT A FASHION STORY IS (AND WHY IT'S IMPORTANT)

Earlier in the book, I spoke about the ways personal style serves as an expression of who we are to the world around us. Well, a wedding fashion story takes this idea and amplifies it while at the same time combining it with the overarching vision that you have for your wedding (and the events leading up to it). To use an analogy, if your style is the exact coordinates on a map, the fashion story is the 10,000-foot view from above. By getting a sense of what you want the full story to look like, you will be able to formulate a clear and concise fashion plan for each event. It also becomes much less stressful. Since you already did the work to get to know your style and the different elements of your personality, this should be a somewhat easy task for you.

Generally speaking, there are three different types of fashion stories that we help our clients tell.

Diverse

This is the perfect story for you if you want to express different sides of your personality for each event and want to combine a different set of looks. For example, I have some brides who want a modern feeling one night, a romantic feeling the next, and a glamorous one for the next.

On-Brand

This is the choice for you if you have a core style that you love and feel confident in and want every outfit to reflect it and work together seamlessly.

Thematic

If you like the idea of a theme running through all of your outfits that culminates in the wedding dress, this is perfect for you. Though most often done for destination weddings, we have done it for local ones too. An example of this is using lace in all of the outfits that you wear, culminating in an all-lace wedding gown.

Regardless of which direction you want to go in, the foundation that we come back to over and over again is *your style, body shape, and comfort level.* Once the dress or outfit checks all three of those boxes, you consider the venue and vibe of each event and what the weather will most likely be like that day.

CONSIDER COLOR

White All Weekend?

Another decision you need to make is whether you want to wear white all weekend. This is a trend that has become increasingly popular, and many of my brides choose to follow it because it feels the most celebratory to them. Sometimes they interject things like a floral pattern that's based on white or even a pattern with a specific color that is part of the wedding theme.

Pros and Cons of All-White

A pro of wearing all-white is that it significantly narrows down the options you have to choose from and forces you to focus while you are shopping. However, this can quickly become a con if you can't find something that you like. Another pro is that it feels the most "bridal," and it's your weekend to celebrate being a bride. But on the other hand, it's a big investment, as white

Lessons from a Real Bride

When it came to planning for her wedding, Lucy knew exactly what she wanted to wear down the aisle—it was the other six events that threw her into a panic. "I didn't really know what a fashion story was, but I knew I needed to dress for multiple events, and it was stressful, to say the least," she says. Not wanting to wear white for every event, which she found "redundant," she wanted to find looks that matched each individual event's theme and looked "bridal" but not like she was trying too hard.

"When we think 'bride' we automatically think white or cream, but that felt really boring to me," she says. After spending "countless hours online and stressing in department stores," she read a tip on The Stylish Bride® about the importance of creating a wedding wardrobe and decided to rethink her approach. "I loved Julie's advice to think about your Style Cocktail and use that as a guide. I decided to play on that and bought outfits in fun metallics and white and cream ensembles with gold and silver accents," she says.

The final looks were all glamorous (one of her core components), and the pictures of each event flowed seamlessly—without a ton of effort.

isn't a practical color or one many women wear year-round. It's also a hard no to wear to someone else's wedding, so you are limited in future usability. As a side note, regardless of what you choose, guests should avoid wearing white or cream to any wedding events so as not to make the bride feel they are trying to "steal her thunder."

Alternative Options to All-White

Alternatives to doing this are doing items in color or patterns or separates where only one piece is white. Typically these pieces are easier to wear again (and also easier to find). You do run the risk of getting overwhelmed by the choices, so think about your wedding fashion story and the shapes and styles you want before you go shopping.

For example, you may want a beautiful suit, *à la* Jade Jagger, for one event and an Audrey Hepburn–inspired A-line for another. Create a mood board of shapes and ideas and then see what you can find in white or cream.

How to Visualize

At The Stylish Bride®, we put together a lookbook (which is a shoppable deck of recommendations) for each of our clients. We include visuals for each event's venue, colors, details, and inspiration. We then suggest carefully chosen pieces that work for the woman and the setting. Once the fashion items have been selected, they are accessorized, and the look is finalized. Not only is this a fantastic way to see all of the pieces come together, but it also keeps you organized and focused. We have included a template for you to create one for yourself on the website, but you can also use Google Slides or Canva.

EVENTS IN A WEDDING FASHION STORY

As I mentioned earlier, a wedding fashion story places a sartorial thread through all of the events of your wedding weekend, pulling them together into one cohesive look. It's important to note that while you will likely have other wedding events, such as an engagement party, bridal shower, and bachelorette party, they are not usually mentioned in our fashion stories. You can, of course, add them in on your own, but I will focus on the main events here.

The Family Dinner

These days, weddings are often multiday events, and this is especially true when guests are traveling to a destination wedding. The first event is usually a family dinner, where both sides come together to celebrate the couple. It's a fun moment to connect—and to enjoy a fashion moment! You can go as formal or informal as you'd like, but most brides tend to use it as an opportunity to wear something they really love that isn't appropriate for the other events.

A great example of this is a recent client who was having a family dinner on the Wednesday night before the wedding and was so excited about kicking things off that she wore a long white wedding dress from BHLDN that she had fallen in love with. It was too casual for the wedding because it was a cotton damask and her wedding was black tie, but it was perfect for her that night. And the best part is, we plan to make it tea-length so she can wear it to summer parties in the future!

The Welcome Party

Welcome parties are increasingly common and usually the most celebratory event in the lead-up to the big day. It is typically the first event of the weekend that brings all of your guests together and sets the tone for what is to come. We love to see our brides kick things off with a fabulous outfit that is fun and celebratory. This is often the event where our adventurous clients choose to wear something a little out of the box and that expresses a different side of their personality.

One of my favorite welcome party looks that I ever did was for a bride getting married at an amazing Wyoming ranch. On Thursday night, they held a "Creekside Wyoming Welcome Party" where the guests came in jeans and boots. We wanted to do something special for the bride that would be in line with the amazing setting and guest attire. I found an absolutely perfect blue leather strapless dress and paired it with a western belt and cowboy boots. It was unexpected and fun, and she looked perfect.

Lawn Games or Sporting Events

Many of my clients who are athletes love to have an afternoon activity that revolves around sports. This could be anything from cornhole to croquet, golf, skeet shooting, or flag football. Regardless of the type of game, there will be photos taken, and you'll want to look cute, even if that means breaking out your best Lululemon.

The Bridesmaid Luncheon

Different from a shower, a bridesmaid luncheon has become increasingly popular, and it's a lovely way to connect with your ladies and have some girl time. It is usually held the day before the wedding and is typically on the more girly, feminine, and romantic side in terms of style. This is a great time to pull florals, lace, or ruffles into your attire, but if you are more streamlined and not girly, go with what makes you feel comfortable. I've seen brides wear cool jumpsuits and pantsuits at these events as well.

Over the years I've done many fantastic looks for this party, but one of my favorites was for a client whose bridesmaid luncheon was on Valentine's Day. We found a stunning short red dress that had hearts embroidered on it. It was gorgeous! Another client had her bridesmaid luncheon at Bouchon Bakery in Napa Valley and loved red flowers, so they were incorporated into the overall decor. We found a stunning sweater dress for the occasion. White with red flowers, it was also the baby-doll shape she favored. It is about having fun with the colors, shapes, and styles that feel most right to you.

The Rehearsal Dinner

Traditionally, the rehearsal dinner was a small affair for just family and the wedding party after they were done rehearsing for the ceremony. Sometimes our clients keep it as that, others open it up to everyone invited to the wedding, and some just include the wedding party and out-of-town guests. Whichever direction you choose, when it comes to formality, this is second only to the wedding, so you are going to want a very special outfit. It's not uncommon for there to be a photographer and videographer (which is a good idea, since it's the time when everyone gives their speeches). Not only do you want your outfit to be festive and fabulous, but you also want it to look great from the waist up because you are going to spend a lot of time sitting at the table while people toast you.

The amazing looks that we've put together for rehearsal dinners run the gamut and are as individual as the events themselves. One of my favorites that we did recently was for a bride who planned to wear a gorgeous beaded ball gown for the wedding and wanted to do the opposite for the rehearsal dinner. We showed her a high-neck, open-back sheath dress that had floral embroidery on the back straps and amazing detachable "wings" of tulle coming off the shoulders. These wings were dramatic and gorgeous in photos and also gave her the feeling of wearing a veil as she did the rehearsal. It was great because we could arrange the wings as if they were the veil when she was going down the aisle and could practice how she was going to position it when she sat down during the ceremony.

If you want to wear white, a tip that may help you when you are shopping is to not rule out wedding dresses themselves. There are so many great online resources at all different price points, so just because it's listed as a wedding dress, it doesn't mean it's going to be a budget buster.

The Dancing Dress

As I mentioned earlier in the book, nearly all of our clients change their dress when serious dancing starts. The list of fabulous afterparty dresses that we've done over the years is long and varies from custom beaded fringe gowns to slinky bias-cut silk sheaths to two-piece pant/top sets. While 99 percent of our clients stay in white or silver, there have been times when brides have deviated from this, and it worked out beautifully.

I once did a gorgeous long magenta velvet gown for a bride whose wedding was at a very cool SoHo loft, and she looked breathtaking. She changed her hair to a gorgeous side-swept curly ponytail and wore a dark red lip. It is still etched in my memory as one of the most stunning looks we ever did.

The Afterparty Outfit

I spoke on this before, but I'm not a fan of doing a ton of outfit changes on the wedding night. This is because each change takes time out of your night, and that's time you don't get back. Our goal is always to be as fast and efficient as possible when we are working on-site, but the reality is you have to budget at least twenty minutes for every outfit change. So if you opted not to do a dancing dress for your reception but have an afterparty following the wedding, it works well.

Typically, afterparties are much more casual and fun and you can get creative with them. I've done countless sparkly short dresses and also things like a white denim overall dress number, a pajama-style silk set, and a bathing suit with a cover-up over it so the bride could go in the ocean during the beach bonfire. Whatever you decide, have fun with it!

Morning-After Brunch

This is by far the wedding event that has the lowest fashion priority. That said, most brides still want to look nice. Chances are, you're going to be exhausted and want to throw on something comfortable, but then again, I have had many brides also wake up early to have hair and makeup done for the event. What you wear will depend on your setting and your priorities, but my advice is, one way or the other, to have a plan.

This is a great time to throw on an easy-breezy sundress that looks polished but requires little effort. Some of my clients who wore white all weekend use this as their moment to wear color since they are now married. I've had people do light blue or floral dresses that paired well with cute sneakers—something I suggest because, if the previous night's party was good, your feet will hurt (even if you take my shoe advice)!

OTHER PHOTO-OP EVENTS OUTSIDE OF THE WEDDING WEEKEND

Now let's talk about some other fashion moments that you may or may not want to incorporate into your fashion story but will surely want to look great for.

The Engagement Party

As this is the first time the bride-to-be has an opportunity to wear white (and everyone else knows not to wear it), many of my clients opt to wear something special but not necessarily formal or bridal. It depends on your venue, the time of year, and the dress code, but you can never go wrong with a great cocktail dress, especially if you have fun with it.

I have seen some brides wear really great pantsuits and even gorgeous two-pieces. One of my all-time favorite looks was a custom white feather skirt that we did for a bride who was

PORSCHE
JUN
CALIFORNIA
N542A0

having a formal engagement party at home. It had a satin-wrapped strapless bodice on top, and it was truly fabulous. It really set the tone for what was to come! Also, don't feel pressured to wear white if you're not feeling it. I wore black to my engagement party in 2001 and have zero regrets.

Engagement Photos

Engagement photos are used for a lot of different things: the save the date cards, the wedding website, the newspaper announcement, the list goes on. Not only will you want to make sure you wear something timeless and beautiful, but you will also want to look like your most authentic self. I encourage you to choose an outfit (or three) that expresses your personality and makes you feel confident and gorgeous.

The first step will be to work with your photographer to agree on the length of the shoot and how many outfit changes you will have (if any at all). From there, you decide what you are wearing and then coordinate your look(s) with your fiancé's.

This can be particularly hard to do, so here are my tips.

Number of looks: Our clients tend to do either one look or three with varying levels of formality. Yes, you have to spend more time coordinating, and you will need to think of where you are

going to change (hint: Pop-up tents come in very handy), but you end up with more options to choose from, and it's great if you are going to be using photos for several items.

Environment: Most engagement shoots happen outside, and I'm a big believer in your attire complementing your surroundings in these situations. For example, we did a shoot with a client who was going to be walking around the West Village in New York City. Think old buildings, cobblestone streets, and cool nooks to pop into. The client had a glamorous but casual style, so we did "downtown chic" looks for the shoot. Her outfits consisted of separates including jeans, booties, a stylish sweater, leather pants, a blazer, a great heel, and fabulous accessories. We mixed and matched and played around until we got it just right!

Patterns: As a rule of thumb, I advise that you avoid patterns because they can appear busy and chaotic in some environments. Admittedly, there is an exception to every rule, and one of my favorite shoots had a bride in a gorgeous neutral floral-pattern dress that looked stunning in the photos. If you do decide to chart your own course, just make sure that the pattern complements your surroundings and isn't too busy or bold.

Colors: Bright, bold colors tend to photograph well, as do darker neutrals (black, navy, gray), and of course, I also love a clean bridal palette of white or cream. I would suggest taking photos of yourself in different colors you like (in good lighting) and seeing how each fits with your skin tone and hair color.

Coordinating: Coordinating your fiancé's looks with your own can be difficult, particularly if they hate to shop. The best way to navigate this is to put what you have selected in a slide deck along with the location inspiration, and take photos of what your fiancé has in their closet that might work. You should be able to get a good number of options by doing this because, again, we want it to look like your authentic self. From there, you can decide what pieces you need to fill in to complete their looks.

The day before the shoot, steam or press each outfit and organize the outfits together. Add your accessories, undergarments, and shoes and put them in a plastic bag on the hanger. Label them by shot and have your fiancé do the same. This will save you tons of valuable time while you are on-site.

A Couple of Tips: I would recommend that you consider having your hair and makeup done for your shoot. I really think it's an important investment, as it will ensure you look polished. Also, you may want to invest in a few pretty umbrellas in case it rains. Those shots can be beautiful—but not with a massive golf umbrella with a company logo on it!

Bridal Shower

Much like the bridesmaid luncheon on the wedding weekend, showers tend to be more feminine affairs, and you will want to dress appropriately. Since someone else usually is hosting the event, you will want to understand what to expect in terms of the schedule, theme, and activities. These days, not all brides-to-be open the presents at the event (although when they don't, the old guard can get a little mad!) or make the traditional hat with the ribbons from the gift. I must admit that the ribbon hat is one tradition I love, especially since you use it as your stand-in bridal bouquet at the rehearsal.

Bachelorette Party

My only advice here is to skip the veils, sashes, and "bride" paraphernalia for your big night out. If you want to have fun and take a few photos with a tiara, bride sash, and questionable straw or balloon, by all means, do it. Just don't take these things out on the town with you.

Honeymoon

What you pack for your honeymoon depends on where you're going, the climate, the length of time you'll be there, and the types of things you'll be doing. It's fair to say you will likely have a few nice dinners out, which is a great time to re-wear some of the dresses that you purchased for your wedding events.

Lessons from a Real Bride

When thinking about creative ways you can re-wear your wedding attire, my all-time favorite story is actually from my mom. She married my dad in 1971, and needless to say, most weddings were nothing like they are today. They had a small wedding party with just a few people on each side (for which the ladies wore long dresses with hats and the men wore blue tuxedos—no joke!). After the ceremony, they had lunch at their favorite restaurant, and afterward they left directly for their honeymoon on Cape Cod.

Anyway, my mom bought a dress that she absolutely loved and has really fond memories of wearing. After the wedding, it didn't even occur to her to have her dressed preserved. That was a good thing in this situation, because for their first five anniversaries, she put on the dress and shared a dance with my dad.

I love that story and think it's an amazing way to relive that day just a bit.

Perhaps what you wore to the bridesmaid luncheon would be nice for a night out on your honeymoon, only with different accessories. Of course, the climate would have to be similar on your honeymoon, but I find that most of my clients find a way to rewear at least one piece.

Here are some ideas for how you can rewear your favorite pieces again:

- Wear your engagement party dress for a night out on the town on your honeymoon.
- Pop on your reception dress for dancing while abroad.
- Why not wear the dress you wore to your bridesmaid luncheon for sightseeing and a nice lunch? Pair with cute flats and a casual bag, and you will have a whole other look.

WEDDING PARTY AND FAMILY

In the next couple chapters, we will get into the "how-to" of putting their looks together, but I wanted to take a moment here to mention that your wedding party and family have starring roles in your fashion story as well!

Coordinating so many different people can feel like a huge challenge, but don't worry; I will break it down for you in bite-size pieces and hopefully even make it a little fun.

Scan this QR code for additional resources from this chapter.

Chapter 12

BRIDESMAIDS AND BRIDESMEN

I KNOW THAT FINDING your dream dress can feel challenging, but the truth is I am not sure if there is any wedding-related task more difficult than coordinating the attire of your bridesmaids. Thanks to different personalities, likes, dislikes, insecurities, opinions, and levels of stubbornness, it is often fraught with difficulties. I have seen it all. From the bridesmaid who refuses to wear a dress because she disapproves of the color to outright complaining on the wedding day, the behavior of friends and family can be challenging to say the least.

Add in different body shapes, budgets, sizes, coloring, locations, and potential pregnancies, and well, you've got yourself a recipe for a bridal breakdown. If you're feeling overwhelmed reading this, take a deep breath. I am going to break it down step-by-step to make it much easier.

TWO THINGS BEFORE WE BEGIN

I want to say this up-front: If you select a traditional bridesmaid dress, your bridesmaids will never wear it again. It's a nice idea to try to pick dresses that they can rewear, but do yourself a favor and take that off the criteria list right now. You might be thinking, "But I found one they all love." Maybe, but they still won't. The reason is simple: Even if you somehow find a dress they like (and I promise you, you haven't), they will always feel like a bridesmaid wearing that dress. In all my years doing this, I've only met one woman who has told me she's worn a bridesmaid dress again. *One*. I am guessing she was in a fashion pickle.

Also, I recommend long dresses over short or tea-length dresses. Shorter lengths rarely look polished in photos and bring about a whole new host of problems you probably haven't thought about. The first is hem length: If they are too misaligned, the photos will look messy,

but coordinating so that everyone's dress is hemmed to the same length will be a bit of a crapshoot (rogue fitters, bridesmaids not following directions, etc.). Additionally, you also have to curate their shoe style, color, and heel height so they look coordinated in photos. I can tell you from experience, there is always one that can't wear the suggested shoe. Bridesmaid dresses have plenty of other issues without adding these to the mix, but if you still prefer to do shorter-length dresses, at least you are going in with your eyes wide open.

THREE DECISIONS

When beginning your search for bridesmaid dresses, there are three big decisions you need to make up-front: who pays; what type of dress (traditional from a bridesmaid designer or ready-to-wear from a nonbridal store); and how you want them to look. Let's dig in.

1. Who Pays?

The first decision you need to make is who will be paying for the dress. Traditionally, the bridesmaid purchases the dress and all the accessories they need to wear with it. However, if you have the means to do so, take this one off their plate. The reality is that it's an item that they might not love wearing, have any part in selecting, or get future use from. Trust me, your bridesmaids will be so appreciative. However, I realize that for most brides, paying for them isn't possible, so just focus on keeping the budget reasonable so that it's not a financial burden to be your bridesmaid.

2. Dress Type: Traditional or Ready-to-Wear

Once the question of who pays is decided, think about whether you want to use a traditional bridesmaid dress (one that is purchased from a bridesmaid-specific designer like Watters, Amsale, or Jenny Yoo) or a ready-to-wear piece that isn't specifically made to be a bridesmaid dress. Here are some pros and cons of each.

	Traditional Bridesmaid Dresses	Ready-to-Wear Dresses
Level of Difficulty	Easy	Hard
Concept Development	Easier because these dresses are designed to coordinate	More work up-front to put together a cohesive look and requires a lot of online searching
Selection of Styles, Colors, and Materials	Wide range	Narrow range—varies depending on qualifications
Fashion Forward	Less	More
Materials	Almost always polyester to keep costs down	Wide range
Price Point	Under $275	Sky's the limit!
Lead Time	4–6 months	Typically click and buy but selection depends on seasonal availability
Made to Order from Measurements	Yes	No
Fit & Alterations	Typically require more alterations because the fit isn't as accurate	Typically fewer alterations needed
Summary	To keep it simple, you can't beat using traditional bridesmaid dresses because the system is designed for large groups of women. But what they offer in convenience, they lack in fashionability, and it's harder to create a beautiful and unique theme.	These are harder to put together, but the finished product is much more fashion forward and interesting. They require much more work on the bride or bridesmaids' part, and unless they are done well, it can look disjointed.

Traditional Bridesmaid Dresses—Pros

- By far and away this is the easiest route because bridesmaid dress designers are set up to work with large groups of women.
- There are a wide range of styles that come in the same fabric and color so your ladies can select the one they like the most.
- The colors also often coordinate with each other, so if you want to do an ombré (different shades of the same color that go from dark to light), you can easily do it within one company.
- The same thing goes with choosing different fabrics—for example, chiffon, crêpe, and lace—in the same color for a more varied look.
- They're priced reasonably so they are affordable for your wedding party.

Bad behavior

Your bridesmaids are the people closest to you. They are your friends and family who will bear witness when you make the biggest commitment of your life. It's an honor to be asked to be one, and they should behave as such. You want them to feel great about what they are wearing, but (and it's a big BUT) you also want them to coordinate with the overall look and vibe of your event. And if you're thinking, "it's not too much to ask that they do this without complaining," you're right. If you ask for their opinion and they give it, it's one thing. If they vocalize their displeasure unsolicited, it's quite another. Remember, if they don't like it, they don't have to be in the wedding.

Traditional Bridesmaid Dresses—Cons

- They are less fashion forward.
- The quality of the dresses tends to be lower because they are made in large quantities and with inexpensive materials to keep the cost low.
- Some designers require a long lead time (over six months).
- Unlike normal clothing, you can't just order your size. They require measurements to be taken to order a size, and that leaves a lot of room for error, depending on who does the measuring.
- They often require significant alterations even though measurements have been submitted. This is because the measurements are just used to select a size, which are based on the largest part of the body.
- It's not uncommon for the alterations to be more expensive than the dress itself, and you have the added pressure of finding a good seamstress to do them.

Ready-to-Wear Dresses—Pros

- You will have many more options, and they will look less "bridesmaid" like.
- These are great for getting that beautiful mix-and-match look that's popular right now.
- They tend to fit better and require fewer alterations.
- Your bridesmaids feel better wearing them.
- This offers the best chance of your ladies wearing them again.
- There is no wait time because you don't have to order in advance.

Ready-to-Wear Dresses—Cons

- Seasonality plays a big role in what is available in the market, so you have to time your search accordingly.
- It can be very difficult to put together a selection of dresses that look good together.
- Color and style often look different in online photos than they do in person.
- To do it right, you really should see them all in person so you know the colors (and patterns if you have them) look good together.
- Dresses and sizes sell out quickly, so ordering can be a challenge.
- Bridesmaids should order two sizes to make sure they get the right fit (and return one).
- Some colors don't have a wide variety of options available, so you have to make sure two bridesmaids don't order the same dress (and decide who gets to wear it if they do).

3. Style: What Type of Look—Same, Similar, Different?

The third decision you need to make is what you want your bridesmaids to look like. Do you want everyone in the same dress, one that is similar (same color and fabric but a different shape), or can everyone wear something different?

You can do all three options with both traditional bridesmaid dresses and ready-to-wear dresses, so this is really about selecting the look you want.

Same dress

Having all of your bridesmaids wear one style, shape, and color dress is the most traditional way of doing things, but it can be challenging if the ladies in your bridal party have very different body sizes and shapes. That said, it is possible to make it work as long as you choose something simple and flattering for all body types. Think A-line skirts, a bodice with straps, and a color that's easy to wear (navy, gray, blue).

With bridesmaid dresses, fabric dye lots can vary, so it's important to place the order at one time so they can be produced from the same fabric.

Bridesmen

When you have important men in your life (aside from your fiancé, of course) whom you want to incorporate into the bridal party, you have yourself bridesmen! Generally, these men would wear what the groomsmen are wearing—or a variation of it—but it's not uncommon for our clients to want them to look a little more distinct and clearly part of the bride's side. If everyone is wearing tuxedos, it's generally easy; your bridesmen will do so as well. But, that doesn't mean you should match the tie to the bridesmaid dresses! That's a hard no. A nice way to signify that they are part of the bride's side is to do a pocket square that coordinates (but, again, does not match the bridesmaid dresses because well . . . this is not prom). For example, if your ladies are all wearing pink, find a pocket square that has pink in the pattern but is different from pocket squares the groomsmen are wearing, if they are wearing them.

If the groomsmen are wearing suits, then you have much more room to get creative with the bridesmen attire. They don't need to match the other men, but they should coordinate. Meaning if your groomsmen are wearing navy suits, I wouldn't put your guys in light gray. It may be fine when you are just with the bridesmaids, but group photos would look disjointed. However, in that same scenario, you may think of putting your guys in a subtle pinstripe or plaid or a slightly lighter shade of blue. The point is, you want them to coordinate with the other men, but it's OK to have them be distinct.

Similar Dresses

This is when the dresses are made by the same bridesmaid dress designer, but each woman can select the style that feels right for them. This is great when you are trying to accommodate different personalities, styles, and shapes, as it is going to allow them to feel more comfortable in the dress.

You can even use this method for doing an ombré of color or the same color and different fabrics. To make sure it doesn't look too busy, though, you want to select two elements that are the same for all of them. For example, they are all long and solid pink, but the fabric can be different. Or they are all long and chiffon but can be in different shades of blue.

Different Dresses

This is by far the most difficult—but also the most stylish—option. By having your ladies in coordinating but different dresses you can put together an interesting and beautiful palette that looks gorgeous in photos. But I want to warn you, it's a lot of work. Pulling together a coordinated multi-dress wedding party requires a lot of time, focus, and dedication. It is not for the faint of heart!

The Pros and Cons of the Mix-and-Match Trend

This is a very popular choice right now and looks gorgeous on Instagram. But before making this decision, I want you to be fully aware of what it takes to get it right.

Mix-and-Match—Pros

- You get a beautiful and interesting look for your bridesmaids.
- Because they can select it, the chances that your bridesmaids will feel great in the dress are much higher.
- They may wear it again!
- You don't have to deal with the whole bridesmaid-dress-ordering process that needs to be done at least six months in advance for most designers.

Mix-and-Match—Cons

- Colors and fit in online photos can be different in real life—so you must see them all together when selecting them. This can be difficult and time-consuming.

Mix-and-Match—Best Practice Tips

- Put the final choices in a slide deck with clickable links.
- Ask your bridesmaids to pick a first and second choice.
- If you are going to take a stab at it, make sure you buy them from stores that have a good return policy so you aren't on the hook for the ones you don't want.

Custom Bridesmaid Dresses

Custom-made dresses are an expensive and time-consuming way to go, but you can also get something different, beautiful, and exactly what you want. We've done many of these projects over the years, and trust me when I tell you that going this route is not for everyone. But if you have the following things, custom dresses can be something to consider:

- **The budget:** In my experience, a starting price point for a custom dress is about $1,800 and goes up from there, depending on the fabric, silhouette, and designer you choose. Also, it's more costly to have everyone in a different shape because each one requires a different pattern to be made.
- **The vision:** Just like with a wedding dress, you need to know exactly what you are looking for to start this project and have a designer whom you trust to execute it well.
- **The time:** There are many stages to a project like this, and you need to have the time and capacity to devote to it. If you don't, you're going to get frustrated, and that's not good for anyone.
- **The buy-in:** The very worst is doing a project like this with bridesmaids who don't prioritize it. You need your ladies to buy in to the process and commit to giving the designer what's needed to make the project happen.

This is a lot! Can't they just pick their own dresses?

At this point, you may be ready to throw in the towel and let them wear whatever they want so that you don't have to deal with it. The good news is that you can let them select their own dresses, but they are going to want to know the parameters, so the more defined you can get, the fewer questions they will have and the better it will look.

For example, instead of saying, "Just go buy a black dress," tell them that it should be a long black dress without a pattern, sparkle, or a lot of volume in the skirt or whatever your preferences are. This will help direct them and save you from being barraged by a lot of text messages asking the same questions over and over. Oh, and also have them send you a picture of what they choose, and pop it into a slide deck as we described earlier. Not only will this avoid duplications (which I've seen happen before and let's just say it was pretty obvious!), but you can also make sure it looks cohesive.

Hiring a stylist is the easiest option.

As I'm sure you can tell, all this bridesmaid styling can be a lot of work. Every day we hear from brides who are struggling to coordinate the look and find the right dress for their bridesmaids. Of course, I'm biased, but this isn't a shameless plug: At The Stylish Bride® we have been doing

this for years and have a system that makes it easy and streamlined. Through our Virtual Styling service we will help brides navigate all of these decisions and ultimately make the process much easier. Not everyone needs this level of support, but if you are having trouble with this piece, it will save you time and money—and avoid taking years off your life!

BRIDESMAID STYLING

Regardless of which way you choose to go, you will need to make a few more decisions regarding your bridesmaids to finish the look.

The History of the Bridesmaid

Today, asking friends to be a bridesmaid is a way to honor your nearest and dearest, but in ancient times, this group of women took the concept of "ride or die" to extreme levels. Back then, getting married was a risky business as brides and their families often had to walk miles to different villages to meet their future husbands at the altar. This left the women vulnerable to kidnapping by rival suitors, attacks by thieves looking to steal the dowry, and curses by evil spirits who aimed to wreak havoc and cause harm. Thus, bridesmaids were dressed exactly like the bride to confuse those with less honorable intentions and protect them along their journey.

Accessories

You have finally chosen a collection of beautiful dresses, and now it's time to bring them to life with accessories. Some brides allow their maids to wear whatever they like, which is nice but also risky, as different personalities often express themselves differently. The goal here is to have a cohesive overall look, and giving them free rein may not look coordinated in the end. A great way to get the message across is by giving them the pages of the slide deck that show everyone's dresses and dropping a few accessory suggestions in there.

Or, one of my favorite ways of orchestrating this is to give them the jewelry you want them to wear as their bridesmaid gift. This answers the question beautifully and gives them something that will always remind them of you and how much you appreciate them.

Also, when thinking about accessories, don't just think about jewelry. Belts, headpieces, and gloves all fall into this category, and a little can go a long way to jazz up a simple dress. I once worked with a bride who opted for a simple chiffon bridesmaid dress in charcoal gray. We had beautiful belts made of velvet and organza fabric, which looked gorgeous and elevated the look.

Another time, I was working with a bride who chose to do custom bridesmaid dresses with a local designer. (We weren't involved.) Let's just say the dresses were underwhelming in the end. The designer

didn't translate her vision correctly, and she was upset by the outcome. Feeling terrible for her, I considered trying to source entirely new dresses but quickly realized that doing that for seven bridesmaids at 4:00 PM on Friday when they needed to be worn the next day would not be a good solution! Instead, I suggested sourcing statement necklaces to add some interest and glamour to an otherwise plain dress.

The bride loved the idea, and I began scouring Houston for good options. Luckily there is a great mall there, and my team and I set out to divide and conquer. We had twelve different necklaces to present the next day and let each bridesmaid select the one they wanted to wear. It turned out great and really did make a difference in the overall look—and it was fun for the party.

Shoes

Selecting a shoe that goes well with the dress (and the environment) is a good idea. It doesn't have to be expensive; in fact we often use the "Daniella" by Sam Edelman because it's reasonably priced, fairly comfortable, comes in over a dozen colors, and has a block heel so wearers won't sink into the grass. Doing this will go a long way in having the bridal party look polished. Many times, the bridesmaids will change into more comfortable shoes at the reception, but at that point it doesn't matter, since photos will be done.

Handbags

I love doing custom handbags for the wedding party. It's such a fun and personal way to complete the look and is something they can definitely use again. While they don't carry them down the aisle or hold them during the formal photos, they do appear in the unposed shots, and it looks so much nicer when they coordinate.

Jackets and Wraps

I'm a big believer in being overprepared, especially since Mother Nature is far from reliable. If there is a chance of colder weather, it's a really good idea to have a coverage option for your bridesmaids. Not only will they thank you for it, but trust me, freezing bridesmaids do not photograph well! I once had a wedding in early October in New York when the weather turned unseasonably cold. The unexpected temperatures took us all by surprise, and I couldn't help but feel awful for the shivering bridesmaids who had to stand outside for hours for photos and the ceremony. Lesson learned! We now always suggest a pashmina wrap or a short jacket that coordinates with their look.

Hair and Makeup

While you may not think about it initially, it is important to have an idea of what you want the hair and makeup to look like for your wedding party. Again, specifying what you want (all hair up versus down, etc.) will be helpful on the wedding day so that the hair and makeup team has a plan.

All of this work will be worth it because, as you know from your own experience, feeling beautiful translates into looking beautiful. Therefore, if everyone in your wedding party feels comfortable and loves what they are wearing, they will be more likely to relax, have fun, and look great in photos.

Scan this QR code for additional resources from this chapter.

Chapter 13

THE REST OF THE WEDDING PARTY

AFTER DEALING WITH THE BRIDESMAIDS, taking care of the groomsmen (and groomswomen) is going to feel like a walk in the park! In my experience, men are so much easier to dress. When thinking about what to have them wear, the first thing to consider is the formality of the event. This will direct whether or not the men should be in morning dress, tuxedos, suits, jackets, and ties. In 99 percent of the weddings I have done, men have been asked to wear ties, the exceptions being beach weddings that took place on sand in tropical climates. This was not only decided for practical purposes (they would swelter in that kind of heat and humidity), but it also looked better for them to be styled in white linen shirts and khaki pants while standing in that environment.

GROOMSMEN

Once you have decided on the formality, consider whether or not you want the groom to match his wedding party or look a little different. This can be done by the groom wearing a purchased tuxedo/suit as opposed to the rentals worn by groomsmen, but these days couples are getting creative with the wedding party looks (to varying degrees of success). Have a look on Pinterest for a bit of inspiration here.

What you don't want to do is have the groom look totally different from the wedding party. This will make him stick out to the point of looking out-of-place in photos. For example, if the groom decides on a white dinner jacket in a warmer climate, I wouldn't just put the groom in it and the rest of the men in all-black tuxedos. Another no-no is to put the groom in a suit jacket and have the groomsmen go without (which is never recommended anyway). Uniformity is key here.

If you do want some variances, I encourage you to consider how responsible your groomsmen are and if they will be up to the task. Sometimes it's difficult getting them to just remember all of the pieces of a rental tuxedo (I can't even tell you the number of times groomsmen have forgotten socks, shoes, ties, suspenders, and one time, even pants!) so you don't want to over-complicate this.

Groomswomen

If you have a woman you would like to incorporate into your groomsmen party, you may be wondering what she should wear. I like it when groomswomen are in the same color as the suits the groomsmen are wearing, instead of matching the bridesmaids. So if the men are wearing a tuxedo, have her select a long black dress. If they are wearing suits, ask her to get as close as she can to the color. But what happens if you are doing a jacket-and-tie look or even a linen shirt and pants for the beach? Ask her to get something as close as she can to the color scheme and have her run it past you (not white or cream unless the bride approves). I would also encourage her to avoid prints, unless the bridesmaids are wearing them, and do the same length of dress as the bridesmaids so they look good when seen all together.

Tuxedo Tips

- Many of the grooms we work with purchase a tuxedo rather than rent because it looks nicer and it's something they will have and wear for a long time. It's fine if it doesn't match the groomsmen's style because it's important to get one you really like. (My husband still wears his from our wedding, more than twenty years later. We've had it updated a bit as the styles have changed, but it's still good to go for the few occasions a year that he wears it!)
- Placing the groom in a slightly different color tuxedo can look nice. Think navy versus black, black velvet jacket versus plain, and so on. Again, I wouldn't get too crazy here with color.
- Case in point, in the last few years, the navy tuxedo has become increasingly popular and many of our grooms have chosen that over the traditional black.
- If some of the groomsmen own a tuxedo, it's fine to allow them to wear it rather than renting one. The varying lapel and jacket shapes won't make too much of a difference, and I guarantee it will fit better than a rental. You can also opt to buy them a shirt and tie that match the other groomsmen so that they look more coordinated.
- If you want your groom to stand out a bit, you could have him wear an ivory bow tie and the groomsmen wear a black one. (Note: This is different from a white piqué tie. Those are reserved exclusively for white-tie events and must be worn with tails.)

- Remember that black tie means just that: a black tie. I am not a fan of colored bow ties as they look a bit cheesy and dated. And whatever you do, don't try to match the bridesmaid dresses. The only other rule here is that the bow tie fabric should match the fabric of the lapel, whether that's satin or grosgrain.
- Another way for the groom to stand out is to have him wear studs and cufflinks that are different from the groomsmen's (who may not have them at all).

The History of the Best Man

Today, the best man is expected to plan the bachelor party, write a fun, colorful speech, and not lose the ring. But back in the sixteenth and seventeenth centuries, he was in charge of protecting the bride from being kidnapped by thieves wanting ransom, attackers, scorned suitors, and even fathers who disapproved of the union. Thank goodness times have changed!

Fashion Tips for All Other Dress Codes

You can refer to page 22 for our overview of the different dress codes.

- **Ties:** The groom (and best man) can have a different tie than the rest of the wedding party. For one of my favorite wedding parties, we chose eight different but coordinating blue ties with varying patterns (stripes, polka dots, flowers, etc.) and then put the groom in a solid one. It looked great! Of course, you can do the whole wedding party in the same tie, which is what most people do, and then get a little more creative with the groom.
- **Pocket squares:** People often ask me if it's OK to have a pocket square and boutonniere at the same time, and the answer is yes; this is a great way to add a little variety to the groom's outfit. One word of advice is that you should have a plan for how you are going to fold the pocket squares in advance. Leaving that to the groomsmen to figure out while getting ready is a bad idea! There are lots of videos on how to fold a pocket square, but for your reference, the most formal is straight across with it just peeking out. You can also do a one-point fold, but I wouldn't get too much more creative than that or it could go very wrong!
- **Shirts:** While you can have the groom in a different color shirt than the groomsmen, I wouldn't get too crazy unless you have the time and wherewithal to deal with it. Selecting plaid shirts that are all coordinated but slightly different isn't an easy task!
- **Vests:** While a three-piece suit is not the norm these days, it's totally fine for the groom to wear one while the other guys don't; just keep it in the same color.

Don't Skip Your Jacket

There are a lot of pictures out there of groomsmen wearing a shirt and tie with suspenders but no jacket (or just the groom in a jacket). I'm not a fan of this look for any occasion, as a tie should never be worn without a jacket, but particularly for weddings. You can choose to disagree with me here (and I know a lot of you will), but I just think it looks unfinished—like the guys forgot their jackets or couldn't be bothered to put them on.

DRESSING CHILDREN

Dressing children is so much fun, as they are always adorable and steal the show when going down the aisle (if they go down the aisle!). The key here is to ensure the cut and style of dress is appropriate for their age—not just in how it looks, but how they move in it. An uncomfortable flower girl or ring bearer can be the catalyst for an epic meltdown.

As an American, I was surprised to find out that in England, children traditionally serve as bridesmaids and pageboys rather than flower girls and ring bearers. They are dressed in beautiful outfits that match in color and style and flow seamlessly with the vibe of the event.

Flower Girls

I have never seen a flower girl who wasn't adorable, so you really can't go wrong here. The most traditional way of doing it is putting them in a white dress with a sash that can be white or the color of the bridesmaid dresses.

You can also put them in something that is unique and get adventurous with it. That could mean anything from using color, different materials, or even embellishments like feathers or lace.

Because there are so many different ways you can go, I recommend looking at Pinterest for inspiration and using search terms that describe the vibe of your wedding (or that you used for your dress search). Maybe that's "traditional," "classic," "boho," or "modern." From there you can decide if you want to look at stores that carry formal children's dresses or use a wedding-specific company that specializes in flower girls. It can be hard to estimate how much they will grow between the time you order and the time they wear the dress, so working with an expert here can be beneficial. Otherwise, you can wait until you get closer to the wedding and use a dress from a store that comes in standard sizes or even purchase two sizes and return one if it's from a store with a good return policy.

Either way, it's important to try it on a few weeks before the wedding to make sure it fits and doesn't need alterations. This will help you avoid wedding-day mishaps and meltdowns.

On that note, here are a few tips so that you don't end up with an unhappy flower girl (which can be adorable for a photo but really puts a wrench in the day!).

- Choose something that they will be comfortable wearing. If they are hot or confined, or it doesn't fit well, they are going to let you know and possibly even refuse to wear the garment. Fabrics should also be comfortable against their skin.
- Make sure their shoes are comfortable. I can't tell you the number of times that I've put a blister Band-Aid on a child at a wedding, and I always feel so badly for them. Ankle socks go a long way in protecting against blisters.

Junior Bridesmaids

Of this whole category, the hardest ones to dress are the junior "tween" and "teen" bridesmaids (if you have them). These young ladies are too old to be flower girls but not quite old enough to be bridesmaids.

They don't necessarily have to wear the same thing as the bridesmaids, but instead, they can coordinate. Some bridesmaid designers have dresses in the same fabrics and colors for these young ladies, but you can also do something a little different for them. I once did a wedding with a large bridal party that included three junior bridesmaids. We were doing custom bridesmaid dresses in four different shades of blush pink and champagne. For the junior bridesmaids, we did a great two-piece ensemble with a pink top and champagne bottom that looked beautiful.

We had them give us a top that they liked to wear and used that as the base for the bodice to ensure they felt comfortable. Their skirts were high-low rather than full-length like the other ladies', which made it easier for them to walk. It turned out great and they felt good wearing them. Regardless of what you choose, it goes without saying (but I'll repeat it anyway) that their dresses should be modest and age appropriate.

Ring Bearers

I have to start this section with the most adorable story from when my son was a ring bearer for the first time. We were walking together to preschool in New York, and I was telling him that later we were going to get his ring bearer outfit (in this case it was a little tuxedo). He stopped and looked at me and asked, "Mommy, if I'm going to be a ring bear, don't I wear a bear costume?" Cutest ever!

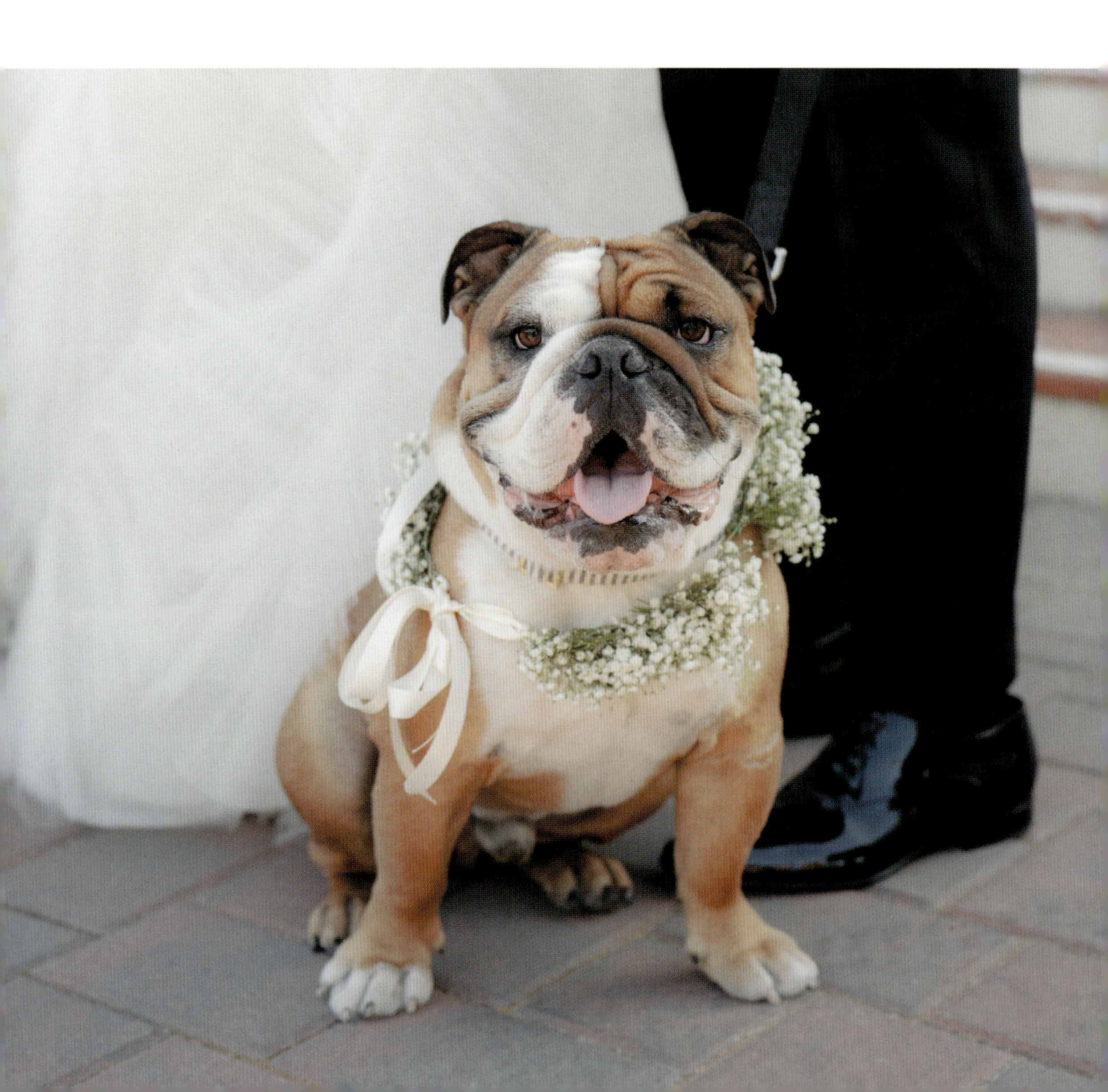

The question to ask yourself here is if you want them to wear the same thing as the groomsmen or something different. I personally think tuxedos or suits on boys are very cute, but I've had clients that hated tuxedos on little boys. If that's the case, you can opt to put them in a pageboy outfit or a "Jon Jon suit" (a romper for a little boy that is named for JFK Jr.). Another option if it's a summer or beach wedding is to put little boys in shorts, a shirt, and suspenders, and it's adorable.

I know this goes against my no-shorts and no-suspenders-without-a-jacket rant earlier, but it's entirely different for children.

PETS

It's not uncommon for couples to include their four-legged friends in the wedding procession, and like any other member of the wedding party, what they wear requires careful consideration. I've seen everything from flower girl dresses made into dresses for dogs (not recommended) to bow ties and beautiful floral leashes. On one occasion, I even styled an outfit for the dog walker who was in charge of walking the dog down the aisle. Whatever you decide, a word of caution: Be mindful of furry friends getting too close to your dress. An excited pet that can't resist jumping up on your tulle dress is a recipe for disaster.

MOTHERS OF THE BRIDE AND GROOM

Mothers of the bride (MOBs) and groom (MOGs) often have the hardest time of anyone finding dresses they love. They have so many things to consider that even the most fashion-savvy women can find it challenging. Helping them is one of my favorite parts of this job because I understand the struggle so much and it is so rewarding to find them something they love and, most importantly, feel great wearing.

When we work with mothers, we start very much the same way that we do when starting with the bride. We consider all aspects of the wedding (location, date, formality) and dig into what her personal style is. The evolution of personal style as we age is something I find so interesting. During our conversations with moms, we often hear about what they used to wear when they were younger and confusion about what they should wear now. I think, as women, a lot of the time we get so caught up in wearing what's appropriate that we lose sense of the things that bring us joy.

On the other hand, as we age we get to know ourselves better and our style evolves. Understanding the sweet spot between the two is really where the magic happens. We want moms to feel absolutely amazing, but we also want them to feel comfortable. This is a critical piece of the puzzle because we know that as a woman ages, she is less interested in wearing stilettos than she is in being able to dance all night.

The other great part of working with moms is that they know themselves well. When you've been living in a body and dressing it for more than half a century, you have a good idea of what will work and what won't. But that can also create a psychological barrier to trying new things, and our job as stylists is to understand and respect a woman's comfort level but also to nudge her outside of her box a little. I can't tell you the number of times that we encourage someone to try on a dress that they doubt will look good because of their preconceived notions of what they can wear, only to surprise them and have them love it.

Just the other day we were shopping with a very chic mom who said she never wears anything but neutral colors. But because of her blonde coloring, we knew red would look great on her. We found a dress that was perfectly suited for her shape and had some of the fun details she loved—but it was red. We encouraged her to give it a try and sure enough, she loved it! If all of the other elements hadn't aligned, it wouldn't have been right, but it looked great and most importantly, she felt great wearing it!

Some of the most common things we hear from MOBs and MOGs are:

- Their figure has changed and they struggle to feel good in their clothing or find something that fits.
- They want to be appropriate for the wedding and also look fabulous.
- They don't want to look *too* fabulous because they are always concerned with outshining the bride (which is rarely possible, but it's so nice that they want the spotlight to be on her and not themselves).
- They almost always want arm coverage and most dresses out there don't have it (a big miss on the designer's part, in my opinion).
- They are often concerned that a guest could show up in the same dress.
- They don't want to look like a guest, but they don't want to be overdone.
- How much should it go with the overall decor?
- Will it look good standing next to the bride? This is something we home in on by whipping out our favorite collage app and putting them side-by-side.
- Will it allow her to wear comfortable shoes? It will be no surprise that we recommend comfort over height, and moms being the wise women they are agree!

A Few General Rules for Mothers (With Exceptions, of Course)

Etiquette says that the mother of the bride should select her dress first, and then the mother of the groom can select hers. I've seen this go many ways, and the politics around it can be intense. A particularly difficult situation can arise if the groom's family is the one paying for the wedding, and you have to decide if that means the MOG should select first. It gets complicated, so my advice is to figure out what makes the most sense for your wedding by talking about it with the parties involved.

Most women know this, but it's worth noting that all shades of cream, off-white, and white are off-limits (unless it's the rare occasion where the bride prefers that), and you even need to be careful of patterns that have a white background. How much white is *too much* white? Always run it past the bride. I've seen some not care at all and others care very much.

Common Questions We Get from MOBs and MOGs

Should my dress coordinate with the bridesmaid dresses?

Our answer is no, but you don't want it to clash either. The reality is that the mothers aren't in the group wedding party photos, and unless you have other daughters who are bridesmaids, the chances of you being in photos together are slim.

Can I wear black?

This is a funny one, and I find that most women have a strong feeling one way or the other. Some women feel that black is not appropriate for a wedding at all because it's a dark, severe color that is traditionally associated with mourning. In fact, every Southern mom I've worked with has felt strongly against wearing black. And if you did this in England, it would translate into a statement of protest against the marriage. Alternatively, other women (especially those in large metropolitan areas, i.e., New York and Los Angeles) see black as a sophisticated color and love wearing it in their everyday lives, so they are fine with wearing it for the wedding. There isn't a right or wrong answer here, so you have to go with what feels right to you. For what it's worth, my mother-in-law wore black to our wedding, and I thought she looked incredibly chic.

Can/Should I change my dress during the event?

This depends a lot on the reasoning behind it and the logistics of the event. It's not OK if the change is just so you can have another fashion moment, because that really is saved for the bride.

This is acceptable if

- the ceremony is in the afternoon and the reception is in the evening,
- the bride says it's OK,
- the wedding is at your home and you want to get comfortable late at night, or
- your dress will prohibit you from dancing and you want to be able to move better (and it's OK with the bride).

When should I start shopping?

This is a hard one because it depends on

- when the wedding is set to take place,
- what type of dress you are looking for,
- how seasonally inspired the wedding is, and
- your tolerance for waiting.

As a general rule, moms should not start shopping for their dresses until the wedding dress has been selected, and in our company, we suggest doing it about six months before the wedding. However, this changes on a case-by-case basis. For example, as I sit here writing this, it's November, and we are working on a wedding that is taking place next December in New York. We had a call with the bride this week, and she asked about the moms. We determined that because they will be looking for winter styles for their dresses (think velvet, rich colors, and maybe some sparkle), we would start shopping this December for them so we have the best chance of finding things that work in the stores. If we wait, it won't be until at least next September that holiday dresses will be back and that feels too late to them.

Alternatively, we often have clients come to us with exceptionally short timelines and who, for one reason or another, haven't selected a dress or have chosen something they now dislike. We recently worked with a client who chose the dress she was going to wear for her daughter's wedding the Monday before the wedding. While I don't recommend this, it's safe to say that where there's a will, there's a way. It's also important to undertand your tolerance for uncertainty, a theme that shows up over and over again in this book because it's particularly important to consider when it comes to the big decisions around a wedding—and the mothers' dresses fall into that category. Not having a dress can be stressful—especially when all your friends ask you what you are wearing—so know yourself and how much waiting you can stand.

Another thing you want to consider is whether or not you think you can find something off-the-rack, by which I mean a dress that's already hanging on the rack in a store and does not need to be ordered. Are you generally a person that has an easy time buying things? Are you someone who is very particular and has had a difficult time in the past finding the right fit or styles that you like? If you are, then you want to leave yourself enough time to have something made for you.

Because moms have parameters around what they can and want to wear (silhouette, color, formality), we often do custom dresses for them. Sometimes this means taking a shape that they know they love and making it in a different fabric, other times this means creating something from scratch (sketch to muslin to dress), and for others, it will mean ordering a dress that is currently in stores but we need it in a different size or color. If you think you may want to go this direction, definitely give yourselves enough time to do it. Six months (or more) is typically a safe timeline.

ARM COVERAGE

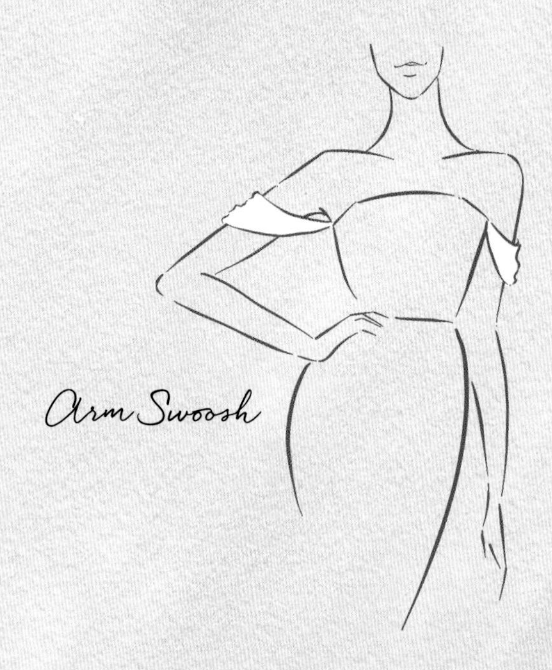

If you are not someone who is suited for the custom route (and not everyone is!) but you aren't coming up with much when you search online, you may want to consider dresses outside of what you are looking for that can be altered to work. For example, because arm coverage is such a popular request and there are very few dresses available that cover the arms, knowing that you can add a sleeve, arm swoosh, bolero, or donut can totally change the suitability of the dress.

On the facing page are a few of my favorite ways to transform a sleeveless or strapless dress into an arm-covered beauty.

Another way you can transform a dress is through the length. If you know that you want to wear tea- or ankle-length, don't rule out long gowns because they can always be shortened. That said, it's difficult to go in the other direction and make a dress longer, but depending on the fabric, it can be done on certain occasions. Could you add tulle at the bottom? Is there enough fabric to let down the hem? These are things that may be possible and can be explored with a good fitter.

Another common problem is a deep V on the neckline of the dress. Most women over a certain age don't want to wear a plunging neckline (and in my opinion, seeing side cleavage at any age at a wedding is inappropriate), so we use clever ways of modifying it. The very best way is to order the dress and have them close up the V when they are making it. If you can do that, always err on the higher side, because it can be cut down later. However, if you have a dress you found off-the-rack and you need to work with what you have, you can look at either closing up the V by stitching it (if there is enough fabric) or adding extra lace or embellishment to the area to cover it. You can even add what we call a modesty piece to the dress. This is a piece of fabric either in the same color or in a nude shade matching the skin tone that is inserted into the bottom part of the V to add coverage.

The point is that while it would be amazing to find a dress that is exactly what you are looking for, the reality is that it rarely happens that way. Arm yourself with the knowledge that some things can be fixed and others can't, so when you are shopping around you know what to consider.

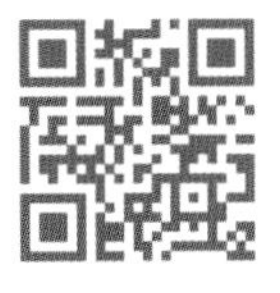

Scan this QR code for additional resources from this chapter.

Chapter 14

WEDDING DAY PREP AND TIPS

IT'S FINALLY TIME TO talk about the wedding day (*Ahhh!*). I am *so* excited about this chapter, as I really feel that every bride needs advice they can trust if, *God forbid*, they find themselves with a fashion emergency on their hands. Now, I'm sure everyone has given you their "best advice" like avoiding alcohol and salty foods the night before, getting a good night's sleep, and making sure you eat on the morning of the big day (a fainting bride is never a good look). My advice is more fashion based.

But before I get into that, I want to start by saying that at every wedding something goes wrong. It's inevitable. Nothing is perfect. If you know this, you will be prepared with the right mindset to deal with whatever comes up. In my own life, I work hard to try and find the positive in every situation, even when it's difficult. By trying to reframe each negative experience to see the positive, you can get through most things. It's all about your mindset and if you commit to having an amazing day, you are going to have one, no matter what happens. Torrential downpour? Thank goodness you have a beautiful tent. Someone spills red wine on your dress? So glad you bought The Fashion Emergency Kit to fix that (I had to throw it in there!). Family member doesn't show? You've found out their true colors. The list of things goes on and on, and with the right framework, you can solve almost every problem and conquer any obstacle.

And if all else fails, remember that the best weddings all have at least one crazy story.

HOW TO PACK FOR THE WEDDING

Great packing is a strategy and an art form and can be done in several different ways, all of which involve a good plan.

We get lots of questions about packing when our clients are traveling to their weddings. We covered transporting the items in chapter 9, but in the box below are tips on how to make sure they arrive in the best shape possible, and you aren't pulling out your hair to remember things. We've also provided a super-handy checklist on our website to make sure you've got it all!

DRESS CARE

Now that you've gotten your dress to its final destination, you need to know what to do with it. The first decision to make is where you are going to hang the dress. Select a spot that is out of the way, free of pets roaming around, and has something high and secure you can hang it from. I don't recommend using a chandelier as they aren't meant to hold the weight. Sometimes a high curtain rod works, but it's a little risky unless you are really sure it's secure.

One of my favorite tricks is using a 3M Command hook. We travel with them when we do weddings, and they come in very handy! These hooks let you pick a spot that covers all the bases and won't damage the wall when you are done. Just make sure to select the size that will accommodate the weight of your dress and give the adhesive backing time to set before putting the dress on it. If the spot you've chosen isn't high enough for the dress to be entirely off the floor, lay down a white sheet, tarp, or even a few towels to make sure that the train is not directly on the ground. A sheet is my preference because it's large and light and you can use the excess to cover the train on top.

Important Tip: *Never, ever hang it on the fire sprinkler system.* I heard a horrifying story of a photographer who did that at a client's wedding. The sprinklers went off, soaked the dress, and the bride came into the store three hours before she was scheduled to walk down the aisle to find a replacement. I'm having a panic attack just thinking about it.

Before we get to the unpacking, I want to strongly recommend that anyone who touches your dress (including you) should be wearing clean, white cotton gloves. I cannot tell you how many times I hear about brides and friends of brides touching the dress

Tips for Packing

- Start laying things out a few weeks in advance.
- Always pack extras (undergarments, socks, shoes, etc.).
- Prepare each look like it's a photoshoot with its own hanger and garment bag and a clear drawstring bag (we use 12-inch x 18-inch) for the shoes, undergarments, and accessories.
- Label each garment and shoe bag with the event name for which you are wearing them. If you love a label maker like me, break it out and get going!

and leaving small stains even after they had washed their hands. You can buy white gloves on Amazon, and trust me—it's worth it.

Now you are finally ready to take it out of the bag! Once you have your dress in its designated spot and you are gloved up, unzip the garment bag and take out the train of the dress. Leave the plastic covering over the bodice and the bodice stuffing inside of it until you are ready to put it on (or your photographer is shooting it) so that it maintains its shape. If the dress doesn't require preparation, it can stay like this until you are ready to get dressed.

To Steam or Not to Steam

At this point, you may be starting to get nervous that your dress won't look perfect after being in the garment bag, so let's talk about crinkles, wrinkles, and creases. It's something every bride deals with (and hates), but few know the *right* way to address them. Treat them correctly and they can be gone in a flash; treat them incorrectly and you can ruin your dress before you even put it on. No pressure!

We strongly recommend hiring a dressing service to take care of preparing your dress, not just because it's a service we offer at The Stylish Bride®, but because wedding dresses are delicate and should be handled by a professional who knows what they are doing. I want to stress that this is not your wedding planner, mom, or best friend. Trust me when I tell you, this is the best money you will spend. However, if hiring a dresser is not possible given your location or budget, the following tips will help you conquer the task.

- **Ask your fitter:** At your final fitting, ask your seamstress how you should treat wrinkles should they occur. Most people don't know how a specific fabric reacts to steam, but the fitter definitely does and can tell you what to do.
- **Try a steamy bathroom first:** This will work wonders for minor wrinkles and I suggest trying this before moving on to a handheld steamer or iron because it's safest for the dress. Hang it in a safe spot, and make sure there is some airflow to prevent water from dripping from the walls, door, and ceiling. Check on it every few minutes. If that doesn't work, it's time to bring out the big guns (and steamer).
- **BYOS:** Don't trust the ones they provide at the hotel or venue (we've seen some really disgusting things over the years), so whenever possible, bring your own steamer.
- **Cover the steamer head:** When dealing with wedding dresses and delicate fabrics, cover the steamer heads with a thin white cloth to prevent water from spitting and marking the fabric. On occasion this will block the steam too much and it won't be effective. If that's the case, and you take off the cover, you just want to make sure that you don't put the head of the steamer directly onto the fabric.

Fabrics That Are OK to Steam	Don't Steam
Satin (unless it's duchesse)	Duchesse satin, because it can get watermarks easily. Pressing is recommended.
Silk	Pleated fabrics, unless you have two people and one can hold the pleats while the other one lightly steams.
Organza	Textured silks, as it could ruin the pattern. If it's a polyester, it's OK to steam.
Lace	Anything that has invisible thread used for embroidery, most commonly found on tulle. The invisible thread is plastic and will shrink with heat.
Crêpe	The satin strip on the side of tuxedo pants. It can cause it to ripple.
Tulle/netting	Men's wool suits should not be under steam for a long period of time.
Charmeuse	
Taffeta	
Faille, although it may need to be pressed	

- **Don't touch the fabric:** You don't want the steamer head to come into direct contact with the fabric. Always stay a few inches away from it. Start farther away and adjust gradually.
- **Steam from underneath:** Instead of steaming on top of the gown, steam from underneath in an upright direction.
- **Check how your fabric reacts to steam:** Even though you have spoken to your fitter and they have said it's OK to steam, we always recommend testing the fabric in the back on the train to make sure it's OK. That way, if you have problems, such as the fabric bubbling, it will be in a spot that isn't as visible.
- **If steam doesn't work:** There are some fabrics that don't react well to steam (some types of faille, duchesse satin, embroidery done with clear thread) and you shouldn't even try. And there are other materials and fabrics that steam isn't effective for, like horsehair trim. In those cases you may have to try using an iron.

Always check with the dress designer or at the fitting, but refer to the table on page 217 for a quick reference guide.

A Royal Mishap

Did you know that Princess Diana's design team failed to consider the way her ivory silk taffeta and antique lace dress would look after sitting in a small carriage for that short ride to St. Paul's Cathedral? "We did know it would crease a bit, but when I saw her arrive at St. Paul's and we saw the creasing, I actually felt faint. I was horrified, really, because it was quite a lot of creasing. It was a lot more than we thought," said designer Elizabeth Emanuel.*

* Sally Benton, dir., *Invitation to a Royal Wedding* (April 29, 2018; United Kingdom: Oxford Films), aired on ITV.

Using an Iron

We don't have to break out the iron for dresses often, but if it comes to that, always start on very low heat with no steam. You also want a barrier between the iron and the fabric, so use a clean white pressing cloth. In a pinch I've used a pillowcase and it works just fine. If the lowest heat setting isn't working, gradually increase the heat as needed and have patience. You may have to go over the spot a few times for the wrinkle to come out.

GETTING DRESSED

When it is time to get dressed, there are a few things to keep in mind and an order in which we like to do things:

1. Decide in advance who is in the room with you when you are getting dressed. There is no

right or wrong, but it's typically family. *It all comes down to the energy you want around you and how each person and the collective group will affect it.*

2. Go to the restroom before putting on your dress and do any last-minute ablutions, such as applying deodorant and perfume.
3. Put on your undergarments if you are wearing them, or apply breast tape, nipple covers, etc.
4. Discuss the plan with your photographer. Oftentimes they take photos of you taking the dress down from its hanging spot, and then leave the room so that you can step into the dress in private. Once you are covered, you call them to come back into the room.
5. Depending on the size of your dress, you may want to have two people at the ready to help you (each with gloves on and shoes off), as you will most likely need someone in the front to make sure it's sitting properly and someone in the back to do the zipping, etc. If this is going to be your mom/sister/best friend, make sure they are dressed in advance so they look good in the photos.
6. Make sure the dress is sitting in the right spot on your body. If they are having some trouble zipping it up, 90 percent of the time it is because the dress is too low on your body and it just needs to be hiked up.
7. Now it's time to put your shoes and accessories on. These make for some of my favorite pictures and provide a nice moment to share with the people closest to you.

Now that you are dressed and ready to go, we are going to talk about the rest of your wedding day.

Scan this QR code for additional resources from this chapter.

Chapter 15

PHOTOGRAPHY AND EMERGENCIES

I COULDN'T END THIS book without sharing some things that we've learned over the years that will make your day run more smoothly.

PHOTOGRAPHY

Gorgeous photos are one of the most important elements of every wedding and a top priority for every bride I work with. But what that means to you and how you get them have changed a lot in recent years. There has been a trend in our industry towards editorializing your wedding and wedding photos, but like everything else, this approach has pros and cons. So, let's break it down so you can decide if it is right for you.

What is an editorial shoot?

Simply put, it's a series of photos that together tell a story and combine fashion, beauty, location, and mood. Every element, prop, and pose is carefully thought out and must relate to the overarching story. Sound creative and cool? Absolutely. Appropriate for a wedding? Maybe. Anyone who has worked in the fashion world knows that fashion editorial photoshoots are elaborate and time-consuming but can produce incredible, timeless images. Knowing your priorities will help you decide if it's right for you.

You only get twenty-four hours for your wedding day. How you want to spend them is important to determine in advance.

Here is what to consider:

1. **When it comes to looking back on your wedding, what is the most important thing to you—the memory or the photo?** Do you want to be with the people you love, or is it more important to get specific shots? Remember, there is no right or wrong answer here, but it is important that you're honest with yourself, as going against your instinct could have a lasting impact. If you care more about the pictures but choose to be with your loved ones, you may regret it every time you look at your photos because they aren't what you envisioned. Alternatively, choose photos and miss out on time with your parents and dancing with your sister, and you may wish you had made a different choice down the line.
2. **How much time are you willing to devote to photos?** The average amount of time allotted for photos is typically about an hour and a half (varies depending on location, schedule, and preference). I've had many clients who hate standing there getting their picture taken and some who have even cut it short because it's hot, static, and makes your feet hurt. But others have loved this part and wanted to extend the experience by shooting for hours or in the days before and after the wedding. If you are the latter, then an editorial shoot might be right for you.
3. **Do you prioritize your photos or guest experience?** When push comes to shove, is it more important to get the shot or make sure things run on time? The perfect photo isn't easy or quick, and delays often happen, which can lead to postponed ceremonies or longer cocktail hours.
4. **Is the look or the feeling more important to you?** This is important to understand because they are not mutually exclusive. To answer this question, consider if you prioritize how you feel when you wear a particular item or how it looks in photographs. Of course, you want to look gorgeous in photos, but is that because of how you feel on the inside or how the piece looks on the outside? This will give you insight to how you may look back on the day. If you look gorgeous but remember feeling awkward or stressed, will that matter? It may have been worth it to get the shot that you love. Alternatively, if you don't have an editorial look but have beautiful photos that remind you of having the time of your life, how will that feel?
5. **Do you prefer a posed look or one that's more "candid" and natural?** Editorial shoots lean heavily into the pose of the model; just look at *Vanity Fair*, *Vogue*, or other fashion magazines. If this is your jam, this could be a great choice for you, but if you think you might crack up at being asked to do that or feel a little uncomfortable, it's probably not right for you.

NATIONAL CITY CHRISTIAN CHURCH

Regardless of what you choose to do, here are a few tips to get more confident in front of the camera:

- Practice before your wedding day. Even the most confident brides aren't always sure where to place their hands and relax in the moment. Doing an engagement shoot with your photographer in advance is a great way to learn what works.
- Remember what we did for the Bridal Blueprint when we went through Pinterest, saved everything we liked, did an edit, and then looked at patterns? Do this with wedding photos and show them to your photographer to align on the vibe.
- Listen to your photographer because your goals are the same: gorgeous photos. You have hired them for their expertise so relax and trust them to do their job.

Finally, if you don't choose an editorial style for your wedding photos, that does not mean your photos won't be gorgeous. That depends on you, your partner, and having a talented photographer.

With that said, here is a very general pre-ceremony timeline so you know what it can look like and how to structure your day. Hopefully you have a wedding planner to help you really nail this down and customize it for you. If not, there are a zillion wedding timelines out there that you can download. This one, is of course, from a fashion perspective and doesn't take into account any of the other pieces.

Fashion, Beauty, and Photography Timeline

Hair and Makeup: Timing Varies

When hair and makeup starts varies greatly on how many people your team are doing and how many stylists they are bringing with them. They are always on-site first as this preparation time can't be rushed.

Dresser Team: Two Hours Before

Our team typically arrives on-site two hours before the bride steps into her wedding dress to prepare the clothing before the photographer arrives. That way when they come, we know that the wedding dress is steamed and ready for its photo moment and the photographer can get right to shooting it.

Photographer: One Hour Before

I generally see the photographers arriving at the bridal suite about an hour before the bride is getting dressed (although many are on-site much earlier than that to scout photo locations or take detail shots) to take getting-ready photos and shoot the dress on the hanger. When the photographer arrives, someone from our staff assists them in staging the dress so that it's protected during the photoshoot. This is really important because sometimes photographers like to put the dress in crazy places where it's definitely in need of someone to manage it.

I once did a wedding where the photographer put a *very* expensive custom dress in a tree, and I had to hold it in place until the wind blew in the right direction and then hop out. Let's just say it was slightly anxiety provoking. Another time a photographer got a ladder and hung the dress from the chandelier twenty feet up in the lobby of The Breakers luxury resort in Palm Beach, Florida. But most often, we are putting the dresses in doorways, windows (I always wipe them down first to make sure there isn't any dirt that can get on the dress), or on a curtain rod. One thing we always have with us is a Command hook so we can really put it anywhere safely.

Also, make sure you have a beautiful hanger for your wedding dress, as you can't trust the salon to provide one. I've seen $20,000 dresses arrive on plastic hangers. Crazy. But I must say, I'm not a huge fan of the hangers with names or "Bride" done in wire on them. Not only are they rarely sturdy, but they can make the shot look busy with too much going on. They can also have rough points that can potentially snag the dress.

It's a beautiful photo to have the dress, veil, shoes, and accessories all together for a picture. Some brides love this shot so much that they actually buy a different pair of shoes for the photo that look better than the ones they are wearing. And if time allows, a good photographer will also do flat lays with the accessories, rings, and other pretty elements. Some even bring their own props to make those photos really amazing.

Bridesmaid Robe Group Shot

We often do cute getting-ready outfits or robes for our bride and bridesmaids, and it can make for a fun picture before everyone gets dressed. Decide *in advance* if this is important to you, and if so, make sure that the photographer is aware so they can make the time for it. It gets significantly trickier if your bridesmaids aren't all finished with hair and makeup, so it may take a little planning.

Getting-Dressed Photos

We talked earlier about the technical aspects of getting into your wedding dress, but there are a few things to keep in mind about the photography side of it. These shots are some of my favorites from the entire wedding, and it's important to be prepared so you can nail them!

Before you begin, discuss with the photographer what angle they are shooting from so you will know how to position yourself for the photos.

They will typically take some shots of you with the dress while it's still hanging and then when you are taking it off the hanger. I love these because it's such a beautiful and intimate moment.

As I mentioned previously, if you are going to have your mom, sister, or anyone else in the room with you, make sure they are already dressed so that they look good in the photos. This is important to consider in the timeline so they are ready to go before you.

Have your jewelry and accessories ready to go and nearby when you are getting dressed so you don't have to stop and look for anything.

First Look with Your Father

Many of our clients do a first look with their father, and I have to say, I love it. It's such a wonderful moment. Most often, Dad (fully dressed) comes to the place where the bride has been getting ready and they do the photos there. It's pretty quick but something that shouldn't be missed.

First Look with Your Groom

I would say that in about 75 percent of weddings we do, there is a first-look moment. There are lots of reasons for this, and your planner will be able to guide you in the decision, but the main advantage is logistical. It allows you to get a majority of the photos done before the ceremony so you don't miss the cocktail hour. Some couples feel strongly that they don't want to see each other before the ceremony, and, of course, that's completely fine; just be aware that all of the photos will then come after and most likely cut into the time you have to go to cocktails.

Personal note: In 2001 when I was married, no one did a first look. I had never even heard of one. If I had, I would have definitely done it because I really wanted photos in Central Park, and by the time our ceremony was over it was too dark out to do them. That's just one of the many things I'd do differently today, but it's a big one. Your photos are the only thing you are left with when all of this is over (except the husband, of course!), and I really wish I had that picture.

Group Photos

If you have not hired a dresser, I suggest you ask one or two friends or family members to step in and play the part. These people should not be in your bridal party and should be able to stand nearby when the photographer is shooting the bride to do the following:

- Do a once-over to ensure everyone looks good—especially the couple!
- Help the bride get in place before each shot and make sure her dress, veil, hair, position, etc., look good.
- Keep an eye on all of the details. They will want to watch out for things that can affect the photos, like:

  Women:

  - The wedding dress hem looking uneven
  - The train looking bunched up, folded, or unkempt
  - An off-center bodice
  - Slipping straps

- Any hair that is out of place (unless a hairstylist is on hand)
- Makeup that is smudged (unless a makeup artist is on hand)

Men:

- Crooked bow ties
- Unbuttoned jackets
- Things in pockets (phone, wallet, sunglasses, etc.) that look bulky

It's nice to have a place to put handbags, and if not, have these helpers hold them for bridesmaids/mothers so they are not in the shot. It's important to empower them to speak up if they see something is not looking good. You will be grateful they did!

FASHION EMERGENCIES

Fashion mishaps happen at each wedding, and trust me when I tell you, they can really derail your day. We hope none of these happen to you. But if they do, we have put together a Fashion Emergency Kit that can be purchased on our website. We wish that our team of on-site dressers could be there with every bride, but knowing that's not reality, our kit is the next best thing. It has solutions for the top 18 wedding day emergencies we have seen over the years and not only what to use to fix them but how to do it. If nothing else, this kit will give you the peace of mind that if something happens, you will be covered.

Here are a few of the biggest emergencies that we want you to be able to troubleshoot if you don't have the kit:

Emergency: You Can't Get the Zipper Up

Use this: A little bit of zipper wax

Here's what to do: This is a very nerve-racking situation, and there are a few things you need to try before pulling out the zipper wax. First, as mentioned previously, make sure the dress is sitting in the right spot. Zipper snafus almost always happen at the join line at the waist because the fabric seams come together and there is more thickness. To see if you can get some momentum over that spot, you want to create a little extra room. Put your hands on your waist to cinch it in or have someone with gloves on do it from the front, and sometimes that extra space will allow the zipper to get over the hump more easily.

But if all that fails and there is no fabric caught in the zipper, take a bit of zipper wax—a white crayon or clear candle wax will both work in a pinch—and gently glide a little up and down the mouth of the zipper in the spot where it's sticking. This should give the zipper the extra lubrication it needs to work.

Emergency: Your Bustle Breaks

Use this: Safety pins

Here's what to do: Hopefully you have a few different sizes of safety pins on hand. Use the biggest ones you have because they will be the sturdiest. Next, you want to find the part that broke underneath the dress and safety-pin the fabric together; pin it an inch higher as well. Then assess if there are other parts of the train that are too long and dragging on the floor. If so, you should do the same thing to those areas so they don't get stepped on and it happens again. If things are really out of whack, take a needle and thread and sew it up so that it is more secure and stays in place.

Emergency: The Dress Gets Dirty

Use this: Baby wipes, baby powder, stain removal wipes

Here's what to do: I like to start with the least intense option and increase from there. We use deodorant removal sponges that are great for removing light dirt stains or stains that can flake off. If using them doesn't work, try baby wipes (always testing a spot that isn't seen); you would be surprised how much they will take off. If it's on the wedding dress, you can also then use baby powder, which not only absorbs the stain but also masks it because it's white.

Best practices:

- Always test all methods in an area that can't be seen first to make sure it doesn't leave a mark.
- Use blotting motions, not wiping or rubbing motions; dab gently!
- Always put a towel behind the stain, then saturate another towel with the solvent.
- Makeup is removed first with scotch tape dabs and then liquid remover.
- Crêpe gowns do well with dry sticks like Janie Stick Spot Cleaner.
- Wine stains respond well to Wine Away and seltzer.
- Have patience. It can take time and perseverance to get stains out.

When—and How—to Use the Restroom in Your Wedding Dress

One of the more common approaches is to have a restroom plan to make several trips to the bathroom throughout the night in an effort to keep your bladder empty enough that you don't miss any of the more important moments of your wedding. I suggest using the following schedule as a guide:

- Before you get into your dress
- About fifteen to twenty minutes before the ceremony

- When you bustle your dress
- Ten to fifteen minutes before toasts
- Whenever you need to after that

But how do you use the bathroom in such a dress, you ask? That depends on the shape of your dress. Before I get to that, let me first say that if your dress is large, it is important that you have a bridesmaid or two available to help you go to the restroom throughout the evening. Having a second set of hands will come in handy and can help you get in and out much faster with fewer wardrobe malfunctions.

If your dress has a large skirt: This is going to feel really weird, but the best way to do it is face the commode so that you are in the opposite direction that you usually are. This is so the train is behind you and it's easier to maneuver and there is no chance of you getting it wet.

If your dress is a snug fit: It doesn't happen often, and I don't recommend it, but I have had brides that need to take their dress off every time they have to use the restroom because the dress couldn't be lifted from the bottom. The whole thought of this gives me anxiety because wedding dresses aren't designed to be changed in and out of multiple times in a day. It opens you up to a whole host of potential issues like the zipper breaking, something ripping, or the bustle coming undone. Try to keep this in mind during the selection and fitting process.

FINALLY, A FEW TIPS FOR ENJOYING YOUR DAY

- **Something will go wrong.** It always does. Go into the day with the mindset that you are going to roll with it. The best weddings are the ones where the bride and groom have a great time. Your energy sets the tone for *everything*. If you are stressed that things aren't perfect or you are caught up in managing the details, then your guests will feel that.
- **Time is the most important currency.** Every single bride I have ever spoken with has said that the day went by in the blink of an eye. After the extensive planning, thought, and love you put into planning your wedding, it finally arrives, and you need to savor every moment. Analyze the cost-benefit of everything that will take you away from being with your guests to see if it's worth it.
- **Eat.** *Even if you aren't hungry*. In the morning, while you are getting ready, eat something light that won't sit in your stomach but will give you energy. Whether that's an egg white omelet, peanut butter toast, or an avocado, make it something that will sustain you for a while. And have your favorite dry snacks available before you go down the aisle—like a few almonds or a granola bar (without chocolate so there is no risk of stains!).

- **Stay hydrated**, particularly during photos. We always have a bottle of water and a straw (so your lipstick doesn't get messed up) with us when we are out doing photos. Dehydration can increase feelings of anxiety and make you sluggish—two things you don't need at any time, let alone on your wedding day!
- **Put yourself in the white zone.** Before the ceremony, I always laugh with my clients about putting them "in the white zone." This means that once you are in your dress, you don't want anyone drinking coffee or red wine near you, no chocolate or berries, and be careful of kids with potentially sticky hands. Once you are married, it really doesn't matter, but if something happens before the ceremony it will add stress to an already stressful situation.
- **Breathe.** I'm going to share a secret with you. I almost passed out on the altar. I was having a panic attack right then and there and didn't have the means to deal with it. It was so bad that my uncle had to go out to Lexington Avenue and get me a bottle of water and sneak it to me on the altar of the massive Catholic church. It was awful and terrifying. I wish I had known back then how to help myself calm down and get centered. This happens to me much less often today, in part because I know what to do. I hope this doesn't happen to you, but if you find yourself feeling anxious on your wedding day, a few deep breaths will go a long way.

There are so many more things I can impart in terms of advice, but I'm going to save them for another time. For now, you have the basics, and I hope all of this information will help you have a smooth and wonderful wedding day.

Scan this QR code for additional resources from this chapter.

FROM THE DESK OF JULIE SABATINO

I HAVE BEEN THINKING about writing this book for the past fifteen years, and when I finally sat down to write it, I made a commitment to myself that I would only publish it if I felt that it was something that my readers could really use and gain tremendous value from. I've made a career out of guiding women (and some men) through this exciting, stressful, and sometimes chaotic time in their lives, and now that I have decided to put it all out there, it's important to me to help as many people as I can.

I often joke that when I started my business in 2004, it was, in large part, to give brides access to information that was difficult to get. Today, it has gone 180 degrees in the other direction, and my team and I spend a *lot* of time weeding out information to help our clients get laser-focused on what is right *for them*. When it comes to weddings and fashion, there is so much conflicting information out there it's easy to get overwhelmed to the point of feeling paralyzed. It was with this in mind that I set out to write a book that would curate *all* of my best tips and present them in a way that helps the reader (you) quickly find and digest the information they are looking for and be able to do so in a way that feels supportive and truly helpful.

We spend so much time thinking about how one should look as a bride, but how you *feel* on your wedding day is even more important. You deserve to feel confident, strong, and comfortable. It's only then that your beauty can radiate from the inside out. The purpose of this book is to help you achieve that by understanding how to turn down the noise, look to yourself for inspiration, and be your own bridal muse. Inspiration can be exciting, but deep down, you are the only one who can say what's right for you. My job is to guide you to that answer by providing as much insight and knowledge as I can. I hope this has been your experience using this book.

If you start to feel overwhelmed as you are going through the process, take the time and the space you require to listen to yourself and connect with what you really want. I'm by no means saying you should agonize over things (because take it from me, that doesn't help!), but rather check in with yourself to make decisions that feel right to you. There is no right or wrong way of doing most things around a wedding (despite the chorus of opinions from everyone around you), so set yourself up with the resources you need to stay centered. Whether that's talking to your best friend, meditation practice, or a great bottle of wine (or all three!), taking care of yourself through this process is essential to keeping your sanity and enjoying the journey.

When you are in the thick of things, it's sometimes easy to forget that at the end of the day, all of this is about the love between you and your partner. Trends and opinions will come and go, but the essence of who you are and what makes your relationship unique is what should be celebrated on your wedding day and always. You are marrying the person you want to spend the rest of your life with, and that is the most important piece. Everything else is just a detail.

So, my friends, this may be the end of the book, but it is not goodbye! I would love to hear from you and can easily be found through my website www.TheStylishBride.com and on my social platforms @TheStylishBride.

Make sure you visit both to find newly uploaded tips and ideas as we publish them. Is there something that you want to know more about? Have questions? Please reach out! Please do let me know how you liked the book and what you ended up wearing. I LOVE to see photos! You can reach me at hello@thestylishbride.com.

Finally, thank you for allowing me to be a part of this very special time in your life. I am honored to have gone through this journey with you, and I wish you a lifetime of love, great style and happiness.

All my best,

Julie

ACKNOWLEDGMENTS

Mike: For the past twenty-five years, you've been my full-time cheerleader, sounding board, and the voice of reason. This book came into existence because of a walk in the woods where you told me to "just go for it," and I could not have done it without you. I love you.

Mom: So much of what I do today are things you taught me, and I am so grateful to you for it . . . the skill of power shopping, the value of finding the perfect piece, intimate knowledge of every great mall on the East Coast, ironing and sewing . . . the list goes on and on. You always told me I could be anything I wanted to be, and you were right! Thank you, and I'm so glad you and I loved different wedding dresses. Without that, I'd never be here today! I love you.

Annie and Teddy: You are my sunshine. I'm so proud of you both, and I love you more than anything in the world.

Brenda: From the minute I met you, I knew I wanted you in my life. I could not be more grateful that you shared your genius with me. You are amazingly talented, kind, and beautiful on the inside and out. I could not have done this project without you.

My Team: D. and Harley, I am thankful for you every single day, and I am honored to have you on my team. You are both incredible women and inspire me to build a company that you love to work for. Thank you for taking things off my plate so I had the time and energy to focus on the book. And, most of all, thank you for believing in me when I went into the gap. You are the best!

Planners and Designers: Preston Bailey, David Beahm, Marcy Blum, Sofia Crokos, Lynn Easton, Deborah Farley, Tara Fay, Jacin Fitzgerald, Tara Guerard, Jes Gordon, Dawson Haynes, Alison Hotchkiss, Lindsey Landman, Ed Libby, Heather Lowenthal, Leslie Mastin, Christina Matteucci, Bryan Rafanelli, Mindy Rice, Bruce Russel, Lisa Vorce, Samantha Walker, Claudia Warner, and Mindy Weiss—I am honored to work with each of you and thankful for the years of support, partnership, and friendship.

Photographers: Jeremie Barlow, Mel Barlow, Alison Conklin, John Dolan, Gigi De Manio, Corbin Gurkin, Harold Heckler Studios, Eric Kelley, Fred Marcus Studios, KT Merry, Donna Newman, Christian Oth, Jose Villa, Phillip Van Nostrand, and Allan Zepeda. I'm so grateful for your incredible talent and brilliance at capturing our work. Every single photo in this book is a collaboration, and I appreciate you.

Fashion Family: Michael Andrews, Erica Arkin, Alexia Andreopoulos, Iana Brock, Marco Cattoretti, Giselle Dubois, Giselle Ghofrani, Max Girombelli, Rikki Harris, Alzira Hermes, Mark Ingram, Zaheen Khan, Danielle Lewis, Maria Caruso Martin, Heidi Meissner, Alison Miller, Melissa Mitchell, Jessica Niwinski, Christine O'Brian, Lori Santoro, Peter Soronen, Kadie Uretz, and Michael Verstandig. What we do is a labor of love, and I am grateful for your partnership.

Clients: My favorite part of the last twenty years is the incredible people I've been fortunate enough to work with. Each of you have made my life and business worthwhile, and I've enjoyed every moment of knowing you. A huge thank you to Orla Duffy, Trisha Elcan, Lauren Elcan, Cate Elcan, Gail Federici, Maddie Haddon, Taylor Hansen, Stephanie Haynes, Dawson Haynes, Melanie Koch, Shannon McCusty, Margaret Nanda, Anjuli Nanda, Becka Nevins, Willi Rechler, Charlotte and Joey Rosetter, Anthony Serafino, Alex Smith, Brit Smith, Jordan Sweat, Emily Tish-Sussman, and Erin Yu for agreeing to be featured in this book.

Industry Friends: Over the years there have been many people that have made a difference in my life and business that I want to acknowledge. I appreciate each of you. Thank you, Claire Balest, William Brobston, Anne Chertoff, Emmy Collette, Natasha Cornstein, Ciara DeMecco, Angela Deveaux, Emily deSimone, Carl Fisher IV, Xochitl Gonzalez, Monica Justice, Wendy Knott, Jess Levin, Sean Lowe, Lindsay Mann, Susan Moynihan, Cindy and Lefty Novotney, Kelly Patten, Carrie Sartor, Shira Savada, Alix Straus, and Harmony Walton. Thank you all.

A special thanks to Rebecca Grinnals and Kathryn Arce—because of Engage I am here today. The gift that you have given this industry has changed many lives, especially mine. Thank you.

TCC: At every turn your whole team exceeds our expectations, and I feel incredibly lucky to work with you. Stephanie, you are brilliant, and I am forever grateful that you share your genius with us. Thank you for your tireless work.

Nicole Regent: Without you, I don't know where I'd be, but it definitely wouldn't be here. Thank you for helping me become who I am today.

PHOTO CREDITS

Table of Contents

Page vii photography by Jeremie Barlow

Introduction

Page viii photography by David Hechler

Chapter 1

Page 4 photography by Phillip Van Nostrand

Page 11 photography by Christian Oth Studio

Chapter 2

Page 18 photography by Christian Oth Studio

Page 24 photography by Corbin Gurkin

Page 26 photography by Phillip Van Nostrand

Page 39 photography by Mel Barlow and Phillip Van Nostrand

Page 41 photography by Mel Barlow

Chapter 3

Page 42 photography by Phillip Van Nostrand

Page 45 photography by Corbin Gurkin

Page 46 photography by Corbin Gurkin

Page 47 photography by Corbin Gurkin

Page 49 photography by Corbin Gurkin

Page 50 photography by John Dolan

Page 57 photography by Alison Conklin

Page 58 photography by Corbin Gurkin

Page 61 photography by Molly McCauley

Chapter 4

Page 62 photography by Christian Oth Studio

Page 68 photography by Phillip Van Nostrand

Page 71 photography by Katrina Lawson Johnston

Page 75 photography by Kristin La Voie Photography

Chapter 5

Page 76 photography by Christian Oth Studio

Page 80 photography by Corbin Gurkin

Page 83 photography by Katrina Lawson Johnston

Page 85 photography by Katrina Lawson Johnston

Chapter 6

Page 86 photography by Phillip Van Nostrand

Page 89 photography by Jeremie Barlow

Page 94 photography by Corbin Gurkin

Page 96 photography by Corbin Gurkin

Chapter 7

Page 102 photography by Katrina Lawson Johnston

Page 105 photography by Katrina Lawson Johnston

Page 106 photography by Molly McCauley

Page 108 photography by Katrina Lawson Johnston

Page 111 photography by Phillip Van Nostrand

Page 112 photography by Christian Oth Studio

Chapter 8

Page 114 photography by Katrina Lawson Johnston
Page 119 photography by Donna Newman Photography
Page 120 photography by Molly McCauley
Page 123 photography by Corbin Gurkin

Chapter 9

Page 124 photography by Christian Oth Studio
Page 128 photography by Corbin Gurkin
Page 130 photography by Katrina Lawson Johnston
Page 132 photography by Christian Oth Studio
Page 135 photography by Christian Oth Studio
Page 136 photography by Christian Oth Studio

Chapter 10

Page 140 photography by Christian Oth Studio
Page 143 photography by Corbin Gurkin
Page 144 photography by Eric Kelley
Page 147 photography by Volvoreta
Page 150 photography by Corbin Gurkin
Page 153 photography by Christian Oth Studio
Page 158 photography by Eric Kelley

Chapter 11

Page 160 photography by Mel Barlow
Page 164 photography by Jose Villa
Page 166 photography by Corbin Gurkin
Page 168 photography by Corbin Gurkin
Page 171 photography by Ira Lippke
Page 172 photography by Jen Huang Bogan
Page 173 photography by Jen Huang Bogan
Page 174 photography by Christian Oth Studio

Chapter 12

Page 178 photography by Jose Villa
Page 180 photography by Corbin Gurkin
Page 182 photography by Corbin Gurkin
Page 185 photography by Jose Villa
Page 189 photography by Jose Villa
Page 191 photography by Jose Villa
Page 192 photography by Jose Villa

Chapter 13

Page 194 photography by Alison Conklin
Page 197 photography by Alison Conklin
Page 198 photography by Volvoreta
Page 201 photography by Jen Fariello
Page 202 photography by Corbin Gurkin
Page 204 photography by Jose Villa
Page 207 photography by Ira Lippke
Page 209 photography by Jacqui Cole Photography

Chapter 14

Page 212 photography by Jose Villa
Page 215 photography by Jose Villa
Page 217 photography by Ashley Rae
Page 218 photography by Ira Lippke
Page 220 photography by Jose Villa

Chapter 15

Page 222 photography by Ira Lippke
Page 224 photography by Volvoreta
Page 226 photography by Alison Conklin
Page 229 photography by Volvoreta
Page 232 photography by Ira Lippke
Page 234 photography by John Dolan
Page 236 photography by Ira Lippke

From the Desk of Julie Sabatino

Page 238 photography by Christian Oth Studio

About the Author

Page 245 photography by Christian Oth Studio

ABOUT THE AUTHOR

IF YOU HAVE EVER flipped through the society pages or a favorite magazine and gasped at a gorgeous bride in the perfect dress, there's a good chance you have seen the work of Julie Sabatino. Widely recognized as the first and *most influential* bridal stylist in the world, Julie has spent nearly two decades curating bridal looks for an impressive client list that includes celebrities, socialites, and elite power players who count on her impeccable taste, highly-coveted connections, and unparalleled expertise to guide them through the often confusing world of wedding attire.

Today, there isn't a top designer or boutique she doesn't have an ironclad relationship with—*Oscar de la Renta named a dress after her*—but she hasn't forgotten what it felt like to be a bride-to-be with no idea of how to navigate the shopping process. "I can remember feeling lost, confused, and overwhelmed by the options and also humiliated and discouraged that none of the samples fit; I had a real crisis of confidence and looked for guidance, but there was no such thing as a bridal stylist in 2001. The seed was planted," she says.

Knowing there had to be a better way, Julie left her job in finance, enrolled in the Fashion Institute of Technology, and two years later launched The Stylish Bride®, a full-service bridal styling company dedicated to helping brides (and grooms) navigate the world of wedding wear. "I wanted to save people from having the same experience that I had, to look and feel their best on one of the most important days of their lives," says Julie, who points out that the difficulties she faced have only been exacerbated in the age of social media. "You will have so many eyes on you as a bride, both online and off. Add on hundreds of dress options and no real understanding of how to shop for a dress, and a bride can become overwhelmed quickly. I wanted to create a space that offered full support and helped brides feel confident, not just on their wedding day, but throughout their entire shopping journey," she explains. So, that's just what she did.

Since launching The Stylish Bride® in 2003, Julie has dressed thousands of brides, grooms, and wedding party members while serving as a frequent source for top wedding editors. Her expertise and advice on wedding fashion have been shared in dozens of publications, including *Vogue*, the *New York Times*, POPSUGAR, *Martha Stewart Weddings*, The Knot, InStyle, and *Brides*. Passionate about diversity and inclusion, she has held one-on-one meetings with design houses to discuss issues facing curvy brides and developed The Sample Size Solution—a portable product designed to help make sample dresses fit the bride—which has been applauded for its practicality and helping to address body size stigmatization.

"At the end of the day, it's not about how a bride *looks*, but how she *feels*. If she doesn't feel good, it doesn't matter how gorgeous the dress is; her beauty will not shine through."

She currently lives in Princeton, New Jersey, with her husband, Mike, and their two children, Annmarie and Teddy.